ALL THE
BLACK
GIRLS ARE
ACTIVISTS

ebonyjanice

ALL THE BLACK GIRLS ARE ACTIVISTS

A Fourth Wave Womanist Pursuit
of Dreams as Radical Resistance

Row House Publishing recognizes that the power of justice-centered storytelling isn't a phenomenon; it is essential for progress. We believe in equity and activism, and that books—and the culture around them—have the potential to transform the universal conversation around what it means to be human.

Part of honoring that conversation is protecting the intellectual property of authors. Reproducing any portion of this book (except for the use of short quotations for review purposes) without the expressed written permission of the copyright owner(s) is strictly prohibited. Submit all requests for usage to rights@rowhousepublishing.com.

Thank you for being an important part of the conversation and holding sacred the critical work of our authors.

Library of Congress Cataloging-in-Publication Data Available Upon Request

ISBN 978-1-955905-46-6 (TP)
ISBN 978-1-955905-13-8 (eBook)

Printed in the United States
Distributed by Simon & Schuster

First edition
10 9 8 7 6 5 4 3 2

For my cousin Latresha Gowdy,

The first free girl I ever met.

We will never be the same.

CONTENTS

CONTENTS

FOREWORD

When Alice Walker coined the term *womanist*, she did so with a desire to have a word that felt right in her mouth. That felt Southern. That felt like home. And with this word *womanist*, many Black women, women of color, Black femmes, and some Black men named their academic work, their cultural work, and their activist work because it centered the experiences of Black women. Because as Akasha Hull, Patricia Bell-Scott, and Barbara Smith said, all the women were white, and all the Blacks were men. In religious womanism, centering the experiences of Black women radically changed how we understood scripture, ethics, theology, pastoral care, religious education, preaching, worship . . . well, everything. One at a time, Renita Weems, Jacquelyn Grant, Katie Cannon, and Delores Williams broke wide their respective disciplines. They questioned who had a voice, who was noticed, and where Black women's experiences departed from a Black male narrative and expanded white women's perspective. This meant paying attention to Hagar and Leah and Zora and Alice and Toni and Audre. And these expansions were embodied as these Black womanists were—for far too long—the firsts. The firsts with advanced degrees in their fields, the firsts in ordination, the firsts in endowed chairs, and then the onlies and fews. They put their minds, their souls, and their bodies on the line for their joy and for those who would come after them. For us.

It is on this foundation that EbonyJanice writes. We have all asked questions. We want to go deeper. We want to push the boundaries. We want to know what happens when we center Black women's religious and spiritual and activist experiences in new realms. We have expanded what we mean by *Black*, what we mean by *woman*, and what is included in religious experience. When I refer to these patterns as waves, I do not mean it as a recommendation or ending point. I mean it as a description of what I noticed around me. And perhaps as one place to moor one's ship, assuming the waters are ever moving.

It is on this foundation that EbonyJanice writes *All the Black Girls are Activists*. And asks the question that we so desperately need:

What would a revolution that does not cost us our whole spirit, soul, and bodies look like?

I love that EbonyJanice assumes revolution. I hate that we still need it. I love that she isn't willing to sacrifice everything for it. As women too often have. As Black women too often have. To resist *that*—what could be more womanist?

I met EbonyJanice . . . on Instagram. Where she and so many others gather to share their manifestas, work, and lives. Because they understand that these are all woven together. And to have more life, to preserve their lives, to do good work, and leave their work in the world . . . they must attend to their souls and bodies in ways that their womanist predecessors did not. Could not. Out loud. In public. With softness. EbonyJanice weaves her story with those of her compatriots. She does not see herself in this work alone. EbonyJanice writes her story of community. She situates herself among other Black women artists, activists, writers, spiritualists, and leaders. She shows us their camaraderie, friendship, and necessary unity. And their insistence. That they can and must do freedom work with softness, hope, imagination, and dreams. That they are not only allowed to dream, but that she, her friends, this movement are fueled by dreams.

As EbonyJanice tells the story of her life, you will see your aunts, your grandmothers, and your self. You'll hear from your favorite writers, singers, scholars, artists, and places. Because the places, stages, and social media are also a part of the freedom dreams. If you follow EbonyJanice on social media, this is the woman you know. The one who gathers, shimmies, cites, nurtures, acts, and goes on vacay. Here, EbonyJanice invites us all into her tapestry.

—Monica A. Coleman

* * *

Dr. Monica A. Coleman is a contemporary theologian associated with process theology, womanist theology, and Third Wave Womanism; a John and Patricia Cochran Scholar for Inclusive Excellence; and Professor of Africana Studies at the University of Delaware. She spent nearly fifteen years in graduate theological education at Claremont School of Theology, the Center for Process Studies, and Lutheran School of Theology at Chicago. Coleman has earned degrees from Harvard University, Vanderbilt University, and Claremont Graduate University. She has received funding from leading foundations in the United States, including the Ford Foundation, the Andrew W. Mellon Foundation, and the Institute for Citizens and Scholars (formerly the Woodrow Wilson Fellowship Foundation), among others. Answering her call to ministry at nineteen, Coleman is an ordained minister in the African Methodist Episcopal Church and an initiate in traditional Yoruba religion.

INTRODUCTION

IN PURSUIT OF A FOURTH
WAVE OF WOMANISM

"Mama, I'm walking to Canada and
I'm taking you and a bunch of other slaves with me."

Reply: "It wouldn't be the first time."
—ALICE WALKER

Womanism saved me. I was in the midst of a theological shift in my late twenties, and Jesus, Christianity, and the sacred text we call the Bible were all on the cutting room floor of my life. One Saturday evening, I got a phone call from one of the elders telling me to come up to the church; there was someone preaching they felt I would really resonate with. Dr. Renita Weems was leading a session at the conference that was happening there that weekend, and it would be my first time hearing her preach. I don't remember the full sermon. However, I do remember Dr. Weems inserting the Black femme experience into the story, one I had heard hundreds of times and factually knew I had never been contextualized into. This is how *womanism saved me.* I was going through a season where I didn't even know what I believed or if I believed anything at all. Then, out of nowhere, there I am, in the sacred text of my youth, for the first time ever, seeing myself as whole and holy and being preached as worthy and essential. I was hearing this powerful womanist theologian offer plainly, for the first time in my life, that God had specifically not forgotten this Black girl.

My personal walk with womanism as a specific tool for sociopolitical and spiritual-religious liberation and freedom began by just thinking about this womanist preacher and teacher and considering that she couldn't be the only one of her kind. I began reading books by Dr. Renita Weems. *Just a Sister Away: Understanding the Timeless Connection Between Women of Today and Women in the Bible* and *Listening for God: A Minister's Journey Through Silence and Doubt* were the first two books of hers that I read. Let me just say that I had never known a preacher to be as honest and transparent as Dr. Weems was in *Listening for God*, and I had never seen the importance of women's relationships fleshed out as profoundly as they were in *Just a Sister Away.* I began to look at the footnotes and citations in each of those texts. That took me on my unofficial academic tour through womanist preachment, specifically from a Christocentric, theological perspective.

A few years later, I began to visit Candler School of Theology at Emory University in Atlanta, Georgia, to spend time with a friend who was in seminary. One day, she got permission for me to sit in on one of her Womanist Theology and Critical Theory classes, which was taught by Dr. Andrea White. I just so happened to be visiting that classroom on the day that Dr. Monica A. Coleman, the author of *Ain't I a Womanist Too: Third-Wave Womanist Religious Thought*, was Skyped in to lead a discussion. Needless to say, my introduction to womanism was very official because I first learned of womanism through

Dr. Renita Weems, a legendary first-wave womanist scholar who happens to be the first Black woman to receive a PhD in Old Testament Studies, and the furtherance of my womanist interests was led by Dr. Monica A. Coleman, the scholar who gave language to what was widely received as the third wave of womanist religious thought. It is also necessary to note that the friend I was visiting in that classroom that day was Tricia Hersey, who is now known as The Nap Bishop of The Nap Ministry. I want to acknowledge that; it's profound how womanist relationships are always leading us towards our higher and most holy selves, even without naming what that particular pathway might be, even without naming that what we are doing in these relationships is co-creating knowledge.

We think we are just laughing too hard over lunch. We think we are just sending funny *God Is Black* memes through email. We think we are just sharing the syllabus of a class that we love with a friend. We think we are just having hard conversations that sometimes end well and sometimes don't, and that's all, and that's it. We think we are just clowning when we name our future churches The Revolutionary Temple of the Poets, Healers & Goddesses Incorporated and call ourselves bishop, elder, pastor, minister, or deaconess. But all along we are in these transformative womanist relationships, learning from and contributing to the future of the ever-evolving womanist canon that we will dedicate our lives to, with or without these degrees or an official authorization from any governing body. Yes, even before we know that is what it is called. Even before we know that is what we are doing. Even before we know that is what we are becoming all along.

WHAT IS WOMANISM?

Alice Walker coined the term "womanism" in her book *In Search of Our Mothers' Gardens: Womanist Prose*. She defines womanism as:

1. From *womanish*. (Opp. of "girlish," i.e., frivolous, irresponsible, not serious.) A Black feminist or feminist of color. From the Black folk expression of mothers to female children, "you acting womanish," i.e., like a woman. Usually referring to outrageous, audacious, courageous, or *willful* behavior. Wanting to know more and in greater depth than is considered "good" for one. Interested in grown up doings. Acting grown up. Being grown up. Interchangeable with another Black folk expression: "You trying to be grown." Responsible. In charge. *Serious*.

2. *Also*: A woman who loves other women, sexually and/or nonsexually. Appreciates and prefers women's culture, women's emotional flexibility (values tears as natural counterbalance of laughter), and women's strength. Sometimes loves individual men, sexually and/or nonsexually. Committed to survival and wholeness of entire people, male *and* female. Not a separatist, except periodically, for health. Traditionally, a universalist, as in: "Mama, why are we brown, pink, and yellow, and our cousins are white, beige, and Black?" Ans: "Well, you know the colored race is just like a flower garden, with every color flower represented." Traditionally capable, as in: "Mama, I'm walking to Canada and I'm taking you and a bunch of other slaves with me." Reply: "It wouldn't be the first time."

3. Loves music. Loves dance. Loves the moon. *Loves* the Spirit. Loves love and food and roundness. Loves struggle. *Loves* the Folk. Loves herself. *Regardless*.

4. Womanist is to feminist as purple is to lavender.

Years later, Black women biblical scholars would adopt the naming of "womanism" into their theological naming. Womanist theology: a methodological approach to theology that centers Black women, specifically African American women's experience. As I've come to name myself a womanist, I have defined womanism as a sociopolitical and spiritual-religious practice that Black women use as a tool for both justice-making for our communities ("Mama, I'm walking to Canada and I'm taking you and a bunch of other slaves with me") and for ourselves (not a separatist, except periodically, for health).

If you want to know what Black women are doing for the movement, we are dreaming. We are resting. If you want to know what Black women are doing that is revolutionary, that is radical, we are playing and intentionally seeking the experience of bliss and pleasure. We are healing our ancestors. We are doing deep breathing and wholeness work. We are in pursuit of our wholeness. If you want to know what Black women are doing that is going to change the world, we are in pursuit of a fourth wave of womanist thought, and that is our very worthy and credible contribution to the movement.

I'm going to do some very audacious work here by claiming to be naming and coining the language of fourth-wave womanism. I'll start by acknowledging that even the spirit deserves citation, so I want to say that there is no possibility of another wave of womanism without the definition put forth by Alice Walker and without the foundational work of Dr. Delores Williams, who is noted as the first person to publish the words "womanist theology." Without the elders who have continued to contribute to the womanist canon thirty-plus years, ongoing, or without the second- and third-wave scholars and practitioners who are the force behind what I'm considering a fourth wave in the first place, I would not be able to do this work. Part three of Alice Walker's definition helps us realize that sometimes the daughter says something out loud and the mother is able to provide context for her lineage by saying, "It wouldn't be the first time."

I have been in conversation with many other Black women spiritual/religious scholars and thinkers who have not seen this language used in this way either, so I'm building off the deep integrity of my own work and the community I am accountable to. "I'm walking to Canada and I'm taking you and a bunch of other slaves with me." I always sit with the fact, however, that I'm still likely not the first. I may be the first to publish, but I know that inspiration is not married to one person, so I am a daughter of a wisdom that flows to and through each of us—whoever is willing to move when inspiration says move.

I am also taking deep liberties at naming what I see as another wave of womanism, just as there were womanists in the second wave doing deep third-wave womanist work with the tools they had access to. It would be arrogant and dishonest of me to suggest that this wave of womanism, which I'm coining a fourth wave, has a particular set of tools that makes it a magical new truth that the world of Black women thinkers, doers, believers, and healers haven't already tapped into in one way or another.

My unique contribution to fourth-wave womanism, however, is the identification and naming of behaviors that are substantive to this particular evolution of womanism. In this current iteration of our collective sociopolitical and spiritual/religious work towards wholeness and justice, this fourth wave of womanist spiritual/religious theory and sociopolitical praxis emphasizes and centers rest, ease, play, pleasure, and dreaming as valid and necessary forms of activism. A fourth-wave womanist would identify rest, ease, play, pleasure, and dreaming, where Black women are concerned, as the central tools we are using for our justice work.

What is unique about this wave of womanist thought is that while many of us see ourselves as spiritual/religious leaders, we do not see any specific religion or spirituality as the central idea from which, or into which, we are naming a sacred text. Religion and spirituality are tools in our work towards justice-making, but the focus is not on the religious or spiritual practice from which we source our inspiration. Rather, the focus is on contributing to a canon of knowledge around what enfleshed freedom will look like in our very worthy bodies, today.

These ideas are central and not supplemental to our movement, making it a new wave. Obviously, we are building upon the work of the elders and ancestors who came before us, but I notice myself (and other womanist scholars and thinkers in this particular wave) focused on these concepts and rituals as *the* actual work, while the waves we source our theory from largely found the academy and traditional publishing as central to building this work.

In *Ain't I a Womanist Too: Third-Wave Womanist Religious Thought,* Dr. Monica A. Coleman sets up her assertion of a third wave of womanism by defining the waves as generations of canonical contributors:

Wave One: The OGs. The ones who first called their work "womanism." They contributed to the canon by naming and defining the work as a specific kind of religious thought. They saw the limitations of feminist theology and theory and Black liberation theology and noted the unique intersection of their Blackness and their womanhood and knew that Black women's experience with the divine was unique enough that there must be a specific method of theorizing that witnessed Black women in their unique theological location. This wave would include Dr. Katie Cannon, Dr. Delores Williams, Dr. Renita Weems, and Dr. Jacquelyn Grant, amongst others. The primary focus was on Christianity in this wave.

Wave Two: The second wave is the next generation of scholars and theologians who were influenced by the originators and began building upon their work—using much of their same definitions and tools but essentially doing womanist canon-building work here (which is why Dr. Coleman also takes a moment to understand this wave as an open wave, since the canon is still being built as we speak). This wave would notably include the likes of Dr. Kelly Brown Douglas and Dr. Emilie Townes, amongst others.

Wave Three: The third wave is composed of those who incorporated the words and work of waves one and two and began to evolve some of the discussion to include Afrofuturism, popular culture, and technology. Coleman believes that wave two offers the language that wave three adopted but had the tools of technology and the incorporation of diasporic spiritual practices as a center and a norm in its religious consideration. This third wave also began to trouble heteronormativity and heterosexism in the framework and troubled whether or not nonblack women could be womanists or should be considered credible doing womanist work. Dr. Monica A. Coleman is in this wave, even as she asks the question, "Must I be a womanist?" or "Do I have to call myself a womanist to do this work?"

Wave Four: This fourth wave is literally made up of the force of waves one, two, and three but does not center a traditional scholarship in our canon contribution because of our huge access to larger platforms or publishing and knowledge distribution due to social media. This wave does not believe you have to call yourself a womanist to do womanist work but that you do have to be Black and non-male to call yourself a womanist.

A daughter says to her mother: "Mama, I'm walking to Canada and I'm taking you and a bunch of other slaves with me." Her mother replies: "It wouldn't be the first time."

YOU WOULDN'T BE THE FIRST

As I have reflected on some of the trends and focuses of each so-called wave, I have also noticed and am noting the ways that fourth-wave womanist practitioners identify ourselves and develop and establish our contribution to the canon. Essentially, I see fourth-wave womanists pursuing practical applications of the theories that many of us have been studying for years.

While waves before us largely focused their canon contribution on academic epistemology at the urging of Dr. Katie Cannon—as she insisted that canon matters as much as it does because canon will impact tenure—wave four has the privilege of creating large platforms due to the introduction of social media as the classroom and no longer having to be in a traditional classroom to have a dais, pulpit, or lectern from which to teach or preach. No wave or generation before us has been able to use social media in the way that we have. The internet was created in this generation of fourth-wave womanist thinkers. We went from analog to digital and from 3G to 5G in our lifetime. Our generation bridges the gap between the technological past and present/future. It would only be fitting that womanists would maximize use of social media for womanist advancement, thus riding the scholarly and creative third wave into the crest of this fourth wave using captions, reels, videos, stories, memes, and status updates as very credible places from which we share theory.

Further, this wave of womanist spiritual/religious thought leaders also may or may not have a traditional academic background. A tenet of fourth-wave womanism, in fact, includes nontraditional, decolonized ways of being in relationships with the communities we are serving, teaching, and leading.

I have identified, named, and called forth these particular ideas as essential elements of the teaching and lived practice of fourth-wave womanists. Let me be clear. It is not profound that Black women need rest, that Black women need to play, that Black women deserve easeful experiences, or that Black women should have access to the intentional stillness required for dreaming. Overworking Black women's bodies is commonplace. What is profound is that (some) Black women are taking the time to rest, be at ease, play, have pleasure, and dream despite their drive for success, society's mulings, forced activism, and the historicity of the use of Black women's bodies for both labor and reproduction. The intentional decision to push against societal expectations of an external, performance-based labor so that we can access ease in our bodies is activism. All Black girls have to make that conscious "push" just to survive at some point in our lives, and this makes *all the Black girls activists.*

"Womanism is to feminism as purple is to lavender" is very important to the deepening of our work because it is asking us to consider what Alice Walker talks about in part three of the definition of womanism: *loves Spirit, loves roundness, loves dance, loves wholeness.* I'm imagining the emphasis on this part of the definition as central to our movement-making in a fourth wave of womanism. This fourth wave of womanism is Black women seeing the necessary relationship between the spiritual/religious and the sociopolitical by centering our spiritual and physical wellness as our revolutionary movement-making contributions. You see this, very clearly, in the work of Tricia Hersey and The Nap Ministry when she says that "rest is resistance," then builds projects and programs that provide space for people to rest as their literal resistance.

You see this in the work of Shelah Marie with Curvy, Curly, Conscious, who is proposing that creating safe spaces for Black women to play is revolutionary because Black women historically have not been able, allowed, or given safe spaces to play. The work of the spirit is in the playing. The work of the politic is in resisting the idea that Black women do not deserve to play.

We see this in the work of Black Girl in Om where Lauren Ash has built a whole platform and movement around imagining a world where Black women can *breathe easy*. That sounds so simple, but again, if Black women have not been able to exist in a certain reality and then Black women start creating space where they can exist in that reality that has excluded them historically, that is revolutionary. That is resistance.

You see this in the work of Thea Monyeé, who is able to bring the ideas of Black women's bliss and pleasure into every single conversation with ease. She preaches that all Black women deserve to take time to consider and contemplate bliss and pleasure. That is radical, revolutionary, and that is our resistance.

You see this in the work of Khadijah and Zakiyyah Abdul-Mateen of Unearth and Bloom, who consider intergenerational healing, body awareness, and mental health their activism. Resisting a societal urging for our attention on everything else but our healing and our health is revolutionary. That is activism.

And we see this in the work of EbonyJanice—me, myself, personally—through my Dream Yourself Free projects. I believe that dreams are our resistance because when we have space to dream, we get to create from our dreams. And when we are creating from our dreams, we are not always creating from a place of resistance. We are not creating from the place of "I have to do this work because if I don't do this work, me and my people will not survive." We are creating from, "My ancestors' actual wildest dreams for me are greater than me living my day-to-day life teaching on anti-racism—as if being against racism isn't a bottom of the barrel reality since the very least you can do is not be for racism."

I know I'm not the first person to talk about dreaming. Unearth and Bloom is not the first place we have discussed intergenerational healing. Thea Monyeé is not the first person to ever ask us to center bliss and pleasure. Lauren Ash did not invent the concept of Black women breathing easy. Shelah Marie isn't the first Black woman to have the idea of Black women playing, and Tricia Hersey is not the first person to say, "Take a nap." But what is very clear is that we are in a wave of womanism where Black women are centering these ideas AS our contribution to the movement and not as a supplement to the movement.

A so-called fourth wave of womanism is asking us to be inherently revolutionary by divesting from the ways that we have been resisting from the beginning of time. This wave believes, both by theory and practice, that any form of activism that costs us our bodies will not serve us—anymore. We believe that if we continue in that direction exclusively with those tools, we will die without our freedom, still. This wave of womanism is asking of our politics: *What would a revolution that does not cost us our whole spirit, soul, and bodies look like, and how is this movement sustainable if we do not put all of the brilliant theory that our elders and ancestors have taught us into practice towards a freedom now and not tomorrow?*

The original term "womanist" refers to those who identify as both Black and woman. Before we move any further, I want to acknowledge that my location is Black and femme. I identify as a Black woman. Some historical critique for Walker's definition is that "Black woman" is exclusionary of Black people who do not identify as male or female, man or woman, but see their lived experiences inside this definition. I use the language "Black girl" to describe my fully grown self because

Black girl is a part of my sociocultural and political framework, but I mean you, too, if you are Black and non-male. If you see your lived experience inside Black-girl culture but the gendered language of Black "girl," Black "woman," or even "womanist" feels exclusionary, please use your spiritual imagination and authority with me and insert yourself here knowing I mean you too. For those of us whose bodies intersect at the corner of blackity Black and not male-privileged, "This Is for Us."

Further, this book will introduce, to many of you, ideas (like this whole introduction) that may start off seeming too scholarly. You may not have signed up for a master's course on womanist theory & Black feminist philosophy, but make no mistake—every line in this book is for the ones who easily understand what I mean when I say Bitch. (with a period), Bitch! (with an exclamation and a blank stare), BitCH (with a slight head tilt and a lip purse), and Bitchhhhhhhh! (with air snatches and slight grins). I wrote this book for you—for us. On my mama, I did.

All the Black Girls Are Activists is an assertion that simply because we are both Black and female, the layered levels of oppression that we are forced into means that when we wake up every day and show up in a space that does not want us, will not center us, tries its hardest to exclude us, and refuses to see us, the very act of still showing up as our full self is revolutionary all by itself. Each essay in this book is an exploration of various states of being that I would consider revolutionary in their simplicity: dreaming ourselves free, choosing loudness, softness, and reclaiming our bodies while sending shame back to where it came from. We're chasing our wellness, demanding people call us what we asked to be called, and healing our ancestors. There is even an essay where we spend time with the power of madness in our resistance work and ending with the topic of authority because you're in charge, sis. I swear! My hope is that these essays will remind us that there are various ways to do freedom work and that all the Black girls have a right to dream of a radical resistance that does not cost us our softness, our hope, our imagination, or our dreams, and that our pursuit of another wave of womanist thought is essential to how we thank our elders and ancestors for bringing us this far and honor their legacy by pushing us forward.

In this book, I call myself walking us to Canada and taking several of you with me.

I already know it won't be the first time.

I'm glad to know it won't be the last.

IN PURSUIT OF
DREAMING

"De nigger woman is de mule uh de world so fur as Ah can see."
—ZORA NEALE HURSTON, *Their Eyes Were Watching God*

I didn't know Patrisse Cullors was an artist.

That is kind of the "beginning" of all of this. In early spring 2019, I was listening to the audiobook *When They Call You a Terrorist: A Black Lives Matter Memoir* by Patrisse Cullors, a co-founder of what we know as #BlackLivesMatter. She mentions something about her art for the first time in the book, and I had to stop and slow-pan through my memory for some sliver of knowing. Outwardly, I was looking like Wee-Bey from *The Wire* revelation GIF. Like, "Wait. What? How didn't I know this about her?" This bothered me to no end, and I instantly knew what troubled me so much about this revelation: "We are being known for our resistance and not for our living." The "we" was me, and "The Homies" were all the Black women I knew in various industries and are being known, most intimately, for our revolutionary educational work inside our various industries whether we signed up to be in these roles or not.

So I'm walking up 5th Avenue in Harlem, listening to *When They Call You a Terrorist* on audiobook. The author mentions something about a program she co-created to support her brother's dignified reentry into society after he was released from jail or after being released from one of many involuntary psychiatric holds. As a program and curriculum developer, I was extremely impressed with the thoughtfulness and community-centered model of this program. I started to think about creating a family and community-centered program for my young nephews who were experiencing racial aggressions in the small, predominantly white elementary school they were attending in North Carolina.

I had recently moved to Harlem from North Carolina where I was helping raise my two-, ten-, and twelve-year-old nephews, T'Saiah, TaShawn, and TJ. Both TaShawn and TJ were experiencing similar challenges in their school, but TJ was being aggressed against in such a way that it was clear that the school just did not have the tools or the capacity to keep him safe in his learning environment. As I began to strategize and consider various other program models that might be helpful to support my nephews in being seen, secure, and safe in their home, neighborhood, and school, something came over me. I stopped in the middle of 130th and 5th, stood in the center of the street, and said loudly, "I don't have time for this!" I don't have time to build another program to supplement the racist programs that should be doing what my supplemental programming will have to do. But those programs will not do the bare minimum of including us because systematic oppression will always make it okay to leave out marginalized folk and then gaslight us into wondering if we are asking for too much. Neither are we asking for too much, nor should we have to create our own everything in order to be able to experience equity. I do not have time for this!

* * *

I didn't know you were an artist.

My girlfriends Dr. Jessica Clemons and Rachel Cargle exclaimed that to me backstage after watching my first performance of *The People Could Fly* at The Public Theater in New York City. I was participating in an artist workshop and residency and invited my friends to come see it on opening night. They screamed, cheered, and cried during my performance and then bum-rushed me afterward like, "How did we not know this about you?"

That's the kind of question that makes you wonder what you're doing with your life if the people who love you so much that they will illegally sneak-film a performance in a theater for you don't know the tender parts of you that make you who you are. The fact that these women could know me, intimately, and not know that I was also a writer, poet, creator, and performer but knew all about my curriculum development and public education on race and womanism was indicative of something troubling. The same exact thing that bothered me about not knowing Patrisse Cullors was an artist was bothering me about other people knowing me for my anti-racism education work and not the living that makes me feel most *me*. It's the same reason why a lot of white people were incensed when they saw that Sonya Renee Taylor bought a new car in 2020 and felt entitled to know how she could afford something that nice. If we are only known for our resistance and not for our living, of course the world will be outraged by our well-being. "You're an activist. You ain't s'pose to be well. You s'pose to be in the struggle."

I just can't see that as right or sustainable, at all.

* * *

When this revelation really hit me, I started asking my friends, who are all extremely successful in education, the arts, mental health, coaching, tech, fashion, and finance, among other industries, "If you could be doing anything in the world, meaning there were no limits or boundaries due to your gender, race, or economic status, would you have chosen this career?" Ninety-nine point ninety-nine percent of my friends, many of whom are your celebrated "faves," said, "Hell no!" The other tiny percentage said "no" and just didn't add the "hell" for one Black-girl-churchy reason or another.

Do you understand what I just wrote to you? If the opportunity arose, Black women who are wildly successful across various industries would choose to abandon professions that have made them wealthy in order to pursue dreams and goals that are uninhibited by the confines of gender, race, or economic status. My successful Black femme friends would not continue to combat racism, sexism, and microaggressions found within their chosen profession if space existed to create something beautiful and life-sustaining from a place of ease, dreaming, playfulness, rest, and the pursuit of divine pleasure.

Furthermore, as a direct result of the intersectionality of race, gender, and socioeconomic status, many Black women have been coerced into a type of involuntary resistance work within their occupations. From devising ways to manage co-workers' microaggressions to creating full programs to address structural and institutionalized racism within their industry, Black women have been constrained to combat white supremacy in the workplace while, simultaneously, maintaining a highly productive performance level. So, basically, come to work, do the work that you were paid to do, and perform the unpaid labor of addressing workplace disparities and white supremacy for free.

This is how our justice work ends up being forced. *"If I don't create this thing, we will not be free."* This ultimately means that there is no space for many of these Black women who were celebrated across industries and across platforms to be able to ask, "Is this what I really want to be doing? Or am I doing this because I feel like I have to do this? Or am I doing this because being race-, gender-, and class-oppressed means there is no actual reality for me to do the thing I would dream of if I had the space, time, and capacity to actually dream?"

In the midst of this revelation, I had a video on race go viral. In this video, I was narrating the actions of all parties involved in a courthouse protest regarding Stephon Clark, a twenty-two-year-old man from Sacramento, California, who was shot multiple times in his grandmother's backyard by two police officers responding to a 911 call about a suspicious person. Stephon Clark was unarmed and holding only a cell phone in his hand at the time he was murdered. In this particular video, a family member of Stephon Clark stood in a courtroom calling for accountability, while several other protesters surrounded him using their bodies as shields to this Black man calling out those in a position of power to ensure Clark's murderers were held accountable. The surrounding protesters were all white or nonblack, using the privilege of their whiteness and their proximity to whiteness to protect him. I slowed the video down and added arrows and a voice-over to show how the police, in the courtroom, are constantly trying to get to the Black man who is speaking out, but none of the other protesters are being reached for with the same aggression. The video asks for white people and people with proximity to whiteness (nonblack people in this case) to consider using the power of their privilege in these kinds of ways. I also hoped to prove that white privilege and the proximity to whiteness is a very real thing, as evidenced by the way the police were willing to bypass all of the other nonblack protesters just to get to that one Black man. It felt very cut and dried. It was right there in 3D, plain to see. Nobody could negate what we were all watching, especially with the slowing down and zooming in on various things happening in the background. Yet, thousands of people responded with something very violent and negative to say about this video that we all saw with our own eyes.

The violent response to this self-explanatory video, along with all the questions I had been asking myself about "the life of my dreams," brought me back to an idea learned from the work of womanist theologian Dr. Katie Cannon: "Do the work your soul must have." I wondered, *Is this the work my soul must have?* I tweeted, "I just thought about the fact that I may never fully self-actualize because I do not know what it looks like to dream of my highest self outside of white supremacist systems. Which is to say, everything I create is created from resistance rather than from a place of just being."

I was in a public discussion at Princeton during this same season of my life when I heard someone in the audience say, "This is the plight of the Black artist. When you are Black and you draw a flower, it's never just a flower; it's a nigger flower." And I couldn't help but to wonder, "Who would I get to be if I got to create my life from a place of dreaming and not always resistance? Who would we be if we could just draw the flower, and it didn't have to be a nigger flower?"

"Freedom is a constant struggle."
—ANGELA DAVIS

Freedom is the ultimate goal of my life. Freedom work, then, is the "work my soul must have." But I still wanted to consider my life as more than the type of resistance we are constantly forced into—that we are born into. I wanted to consider what my highest imagination of myself revealed without white supremacy as the filter through which I create, build, and exist. I realized that in order for me to be able to get to the work my soul must have, I needed either a new vision or a clearer vision of how to do justice work that didn't cost me my body. This, intuitively, called me to dreaming as a deep, intentional part of my practice. "Wildest dreams" isn't necessarily a practice that Black people, particularly my ancestors who lived through chattel slavery, have historically been afforded the space, time, or resources to linger in. Niggas' "wildest dreams" was to avoid physical assault by Massa, have consistent shelter, not have their family sold, have food, not be murdered, not have to murder anyone to stay free, and not have their rights stripped from them at the whims of their tyrannical government. You know, basic "wild dreams" like that. So I instinctively knew that with few resources and no real language or traditionally documented praxis for what this would look like in my immediate community, "Dreaming as Radical Resistance" was surely about to become a tedious work but a work I was willing to consider.

When Afrofuturist artist Alisha Wormsley placed the words "There Are Black People in the Future" on a billboard in a gentrifying portion of Philadelphia to address the systematic oppression of people of color through space and time, a resurgence of an Afrofuturistic movement was sparked—a movement that has called on other Black people, across the diaspora, to use those words freely to protest, create art, build theory, and participate in corporate and collective dreaming. Black people will be in the future despite how toxic a violent cisgendered, heterosexual, patriarchal, ableist, and global white supremacist society has been to our bodies and our dreams for generations. In the same way, Wormsley doesn't assert herself as the first Black creator to think about the state of Black people in the future (see Sun Ra, Octavia Butler, Parliament-Funkadelic, Outkast, Janelle Monae, Ytasha Womack, and many other brilliant creatives for their contributions to literature and visual and performance art that provides embodied context for Black people existing into the future), neither am I the first person to be thinking of dreams as an actual tool for seeing ourselves free in the future. Dr. Martin Luther King Jr.'s "dream," inspired by the Black femme preacher Rev. Dr. Prathia Hall, became the vision that he insisted carried him deeper into his own work around class equity. Moor Mother and Rasheedah Phillips call us to consider the power tool of Black quantum futurism as a science and an internal, inherited technology that is guiding us back to and towards a liberated future. Adrienne Maree Brown says, "Our visions are ropes through devastation." So dreaming, imagining, and visioning are tried and tested mechanisms by which Black folk know how to see freedom and walk towards that great destination.

DREAMS AS RADICAL RESISTANCE

"Dreaming" is a form of radical resistance because it calls us to a conscious stillness, which manifests itself as ease in the body. Ease, in a Black body, is revolutionary because Black people have not, historically, as a result of chattel slavery, had access to ease in our bodies. Dreaming, however, subverts a global anti-Black unease that actively works to commodify Black bodies. Plainly, dreaming is radical resistance because the fantastic hegemonic imagination (Emilie Townes, 2006) cannot function with Black bodies at rest. White supremacist delusion (Sonya Renee Taylor, 2018) sees Black people through a lens of labor extraction, inventory keeping, and categorization. A Black person intentionally in pursuit of the conscious stillness required to be able to tap into dreams is revolutionary because it resists labor extraction, classification, or unimaginative naming. Dreaming is a tool for global Black liberation because it calls forth the internal, ancestral technology of Blackness that survives and thrives in and out of space and time.

This eternal thriving in and out of space and time is what Thea Monyeé would call "The Upward Black Resiliency Spiral." This spiral starts with knowing that time is neither linear nor married to one location or space. Dreaming allows us to travel forward, backward, state to state, and continent to continent but always upward in progression towards a higher knowing of freedom than before. This means I can use my dreams and imagination to go backward in time to ask Malcolm X, for example, for clarity about how he arrived here, both through the proof of his archives and the gospel of the spiritual imagination (Toni Morrison tells us that the spiritual imagination is the gospel truth). Or I can use my dreams to go to the highest imagination of myself as a free woman and ask, "How did you get here, Free EbonyJanice?" Then I use the clues that Free EbonyJanice offers me to begin creating the action plan for myself towards freedom. Those clues can be as large as telling me to leave the country, and they can be as simple as telling me to send an email. Whatever the clues are, I trust them like they are the gospel truth because they are the gospel truth.

Another way I would say this is, I ask my dreams to reveal to me who I am outside of the gaze of whiteness, and then I decide to go create myself as whomever Higher Me reveals. This is forever work. This is tedious work. The consideration of what I look like, my location, my career, and my relationships—everything is inside this question to Higher Me. I may not come out of the dream with all the answers, but I certainly have powerful tools in that vision that will cause me to pivot from narratives that hold me in bondage towards a destination that hopes me into a freer version of myself and possibly a freer version of my entire bloodline.

In late 2019, I was in conversation with Rachel Cargle for *Harper's Bazaar*. In this conversation, I said, "It is revolutionary to see a Black woman chilling." A Black femme activist replied to that on social media by saying, "Revolutionary? Words mean things, sis." I remember thinking, *Yeah, words do mean things, and I'm clear that the words I just put together mean exactly what I meant for them to mean.* This was actually a rejection of the word "revolutionary" in relation to Black women "chilling."

Let's define revolutionary.

REVOLUTIONARY:
involving or causing a complete or dramatic change.

In this book, we're going to spend quite a bit of time considering what a cause of a complete or dramatic change looks like in regard to the oppression, discrimination, and aggressions that happen against Black women and femmes and their bodies on a daily basis. But this particular argument was that revolution must look a certain way, and a Black woman chilling did not equate to "causing a complete or dramatic change." Here is my question: Have you ever just seen a gaggle of Black women chilling? Have you ever walked into a room and been like, "Yassss, all the Black girls are chilling!"

I would wager that you have not, or you don't often. What you are more likely to walk into a room and yell is, "Yassss, look at all these Black girls being strong!"

Dr. Chanequa Walker-Barnes wrote a whole book about the case of a strong Black woman versus Black women who happen to be strong. She writes that there is an idea that Black women and girls exist inside of these various tropes and stereotypes that assume that we are StrongBlackWomen versus the concept that she's putting forth that we are Black women and girls who *happen* to be strong. The difference is that I am not (just) a StrongBlackWoman and therefore can shoulder any burden or hardship without fail—that is all that I am. I am a Black woman who happens to be strong and also experiences grief, heartache, insufficiency, fear, vulnerability, and various other feelings that would not be described in relation to Black women who are assumed to just be strong. We are various other things, in addition to a strength we have had to learn due to the perception of our so-called innate capacity for strength (also, pain).

There are various other texts that also speak to the different tropes and toxic narratives that Black women are forced into. Amongst those various tropes and stereotypes, there is no image of a Black woman at rest, in her ease and bliss, that is celebrated. In fact, amongst the tropes and stereotypes of Black women "chilling" is the "Welfare Queen," which wants us to believe that Black women "doing nothing" are "lazy" and there is not a possibility of a Black woman at rest, ease, pleasure, or chilling as something she should have access to or that she is worthy of.

In her book *Anything We Love Can Be Saved*, Alice Walker writes about feeling like her activism wasn't enough. Even she went through seasons of her own work as a writer, journalist, and thinker who felt like because she wasn't "marching on Selma," what she was doing didn't count. (That's my language, not her words specifically, as she wasn't marching on Selma.) There are so many other Black women who have dealt with the tension of this idea that revolution must look a certain way. However, in defining activism, it consists of efforts to promote, impede, direct, or intervene in social, political, economic, or environmental reform with the desire to make changes in society towards a perceived greater good.

If the idea of Black women, who historically don't get to chill, is promoted as an opportunity or possibility that causes Black women to actually chill, and the ripples of what happens once said Black women chill makes changes in society, then is that not an effort to promote, impede, and intervene in the sociopolitical, economical, and environmental state, very much causing a complete or dramatic change (which is the very definition of revolutionary)?

Particularly, revolutionary is to be able to ask Black women the questions, "Who are you outside of your work? Who are you outside of this conversation?" The concept of dreaming and imagining must be considered actual liberation, justice, and freedom work.

This is revolutionary because, as noted, there are Black women doing brilliant, powerful, empowering work, of course, that will inform and inspire us deeper into a radical, beautiful, and hopeful future. But that work has no capacity to see the individual as whole. If I am being identified, most commonly, by my work and not by my dreams, my ideas—the things that make me wonder and leave me in awe—am I not just in a constant cycle of still being oppressed, even inside of the work that I'm doing to so-called bring me and us out of oppression? Toni Morrison speaks to this when she says, "The function, the very serious function of racism is distraction. It keeps you from doing your work. It keeps you explaining, over and over again, your reason for being. Somebody says you have no language and you spend twenty years proving that you do. Somebody says your head isn't shaped properly so you have scientists working on the fact that it is. Somebody says you have no art, so you dredge that up. Somebody says you have no kingdoms, so you dredge that up. None of this is necessary. There will always be one more thing."

Nanny told the truth in *Their Eyes Were Watching God* when she said to Janie, "De nigger woman is the mule of the world" (Zora Neale Hurston). *All the Black Girls Are Activists* is about how radical and revolutionary it is for *de nigger woman* to decide she ain't gonna be a mule for the world anymore. "In Pursuit of Dreaming" hopes to make us examine the internalized misogynoir (Moya Bailey, 2010) that causes many Black women, even inside of revolutionary workspaces, and those who are in community with us (or so-called in community with us) to consider why it is so impossible for us and for them to see Black women chilling, playing, centering our wellness, and dreaming as a worthy and credible contribution to "promoting, impeding, directing, and intervening in the current social, political, economic, and environmental realities that keep us from the perceived greater good." It is quite revolutionary for *de nigger woman* to decide she ain't gonna be the mule of the world no mo'.

IN PURSUIT OF
LOUDNESS

"There ain't no future (or freedom) in yo' frontin'."
—MC BREED

My cousin Latresha Gowdy had green, red, and yellow hair when we were teenagers. Before I ever remember seeing Lil' Kim in that "Crush on You" video with all those different hair colors, nail colors, and outfit styles, my cousin Latresha Gowdy was about that life. She also was one of the earliest proofs of my deeply ingrained truth system around respectability politics because one thing that Latresha was, in every way of being, was loud.

When we were young girls, I remember going to the salon to get my nails done with Latresha and my sister, Alesha. If the nail tech was being too heavy-handed with Latresha, she would disapprovingly and often loudly yank her hands away. If they didn't shape her nails exactly as she liked, she would have them take the acrylic completely off and start again from scratch. She would get to the end of the full set and have them redo the whole set if it wasn't exactly what she wanted. If the nail tech happened to speak in a different language while she was asking them to fix something, she would ask them, "Are you talking about me?" And if they ever said anything that could have been construed as disrespect, Latresha was very quick to name it as disrespect, out loud.

I was embarrassed. I was taught, with intention, "how to be a lady." Being a "lady," according to my specific brand of respectability, meant being polite, even if people weren't being polite to me, smiling, even if there was nothing to smile about, talking in a gentle tone, even if someone else was being aggressive, and not drawing attention to myself, even if there was some issue at hand that required a firm tone or a slightly raised voice because "a lady never raises her voice." So why couldn't Latresha just get her nails done and be content and quiet like me? I would look at her in public sometimes and think, "Ma'am, why are you acting like this?" Meanwhile, "Ma'am" just wanted, and deserved, what she paid for.

Latresha was the embodiment of "What are you going to do for freedom today?" Because every single time I saw her, she was "in process" out loud, "healing" out loud, and "on this life journey" out loud. She would even consistently praise God, loud and for no reason sometimes. I could tell her, "Latresha, I got all A's on my report card," and she would reply, loudly enough for all to hear, "Praise God, Ebony!" Her outfits were loud. Her hair was loud. Her smile was loud. Her voice was loud. My cousin Latresha Gowdy was loud.

As I do more intentional work on my internalized respectability politics filter, I realize that when you critique Black girls for being "loud," what you're actually critiquing is Black girlhood, which is the introduction to Black womanhood. One thing Black girls are going to be consistently accused of, just for showing up and being themselves, is being too much, doing the most, or being too loud—a distraction.

Loud is outside of the mainstream's acceptable way of being. Some would say loud is ghetto, but we all know that anything that comes directly from Black femme culture is *ghetto until proven fashionable* (Nareasha Willis, 2017). Long nails, gelled-down baby hairs, brightly colored clothes and hair, and hands full of jewelry have historically been deemed unprofessional, ghetto, and off trend—until those "trends" are stolen by a capitalist mass-marketing machine that centers whiteness as the standard. So when white women start participating in those trends, then it's no longer too much—it's fashionable. Similarly, eye rolls, teeth sucking, pursed lips, neck rolling, hands on hips, and loud talking have historically been behaviors and so-called characteristics of Black women with attitudes—ghetto girls. That is, until a capitalist mass-marketing machine that centers whiteness as the standard, and white, gay men take those very behaviors and integrate them into their public behavior and receive attention, celebration, and praise by trying to mimic the very behaviors that pigeonhole Black women into a harmful stereotype—ghetto. So to critique Latresha's loudness is to assert that Black girlhood at its highest decibel is wrong, but most specifically, wrong when the loudness comes through a body like hers.

Respectability politics are defined as a set of beliefs holding that conformity to prescribed mainstream standards of appearance and behavior will protect a person who is part of a marginalized group, especially a Black person, from prejudice and systemic injustices. The politics of respectability is a form of moralistic discourse used by certain people—usually elders, public and prominent figures, leaders, and scholars—who are members of those various marginalized groups, asserting that to look, act, behave, dress, and present a certain way is to ensure safety inside of an anti-Black capitalist society. The reality is that Black girlhood, on its highest decibel, no matter how loud or how muted it is, will always still be on the outside of the mainstream's acceptable way of being. This places Black girlhood in contrast to the basic concept of girlhood in general.

A few years ago, I taught a Girls, Girlhood, and Girl Culture undergrad course for several semesters in New Jersey. In order to ensure that the actual curriculum included girls who looked like my Black and brown students in Jersey City, New Jersey, I had to build the entire curriculum from scratch and completely decolonize the syllabus. What most published scholars have been writing about when they write about "girlhood" is "white girls and white girlhood." Girls of color, particularly Black girls, were never considered in the context of girlhood studies, certainly not in a way that centers their experiences, culture, and ways of being. This means that, again, no matter how high the decibel, the loudness of Black girlhood in its behavior, or how muted the decibel, Black girlhood will always be considered outside of the actual acceptable standards and parameters of what is worthy of being considered "girl."

Think about sixteen-year-old Shakara of Columbia, South Carolina. While still sitting at her school desk, she was picked up and body slammed by a police officer solely because she refused to put her phone down in the classroom. He grabbed her neck, flipped her backward, dragged her, and threw her across the floor. *A sixteen-year-old girl.*

Think about:

Fifteen-year-old Dejarra from North Texas. She was tackled to the ground at a swimming pool by a police officer, who then pinned her with his knee in her back while she lay screaming for relief—in a bikini. A fifteen-year-old girl.

Briana, age fourteen. After being hit by a car while riding her bicycle in a predominantly white neighborhood, Briana was questioned, thrown against a wall, and pepper sprayed by the police as they attempted to put her in the back seat of a police car. A fourteen-year-old girl.

Even after I list these three examples, some readers will google search *what happened leading up to the events* that I have just listed. This is proof of your inherent and internal bias against Black girls as girls because is there ever any justification for a grown, adult man to act violently towards a child? Particularly a girl child? You will question "what happened" because you subconsciously believe that Black girls might have done something to deserve this. James Baldwin says that the house is on fire, and we all have (Black people included) inhaled the smoke. I hope you will sit with the harsh reality of your socialization not to see Black girls as worthy of the same gentleness and tenderness that other girls receive. What you do with that information about yourself could be your own radical activism moving forward.

WHERE YOU SHOW OUT IS WHERE I SHOW OUT

When I was a child, my mother did not care what the occasion was, what the setting was, nor did she care about who was around. Whether we were in church, the local Hill's department store, or in line at Ponderosa Steakhouse, it did not matter. If we got in public and "showed out" (misbehaved), my mother was clear that, with no hesitation and in no uncertain words, she was going to show out right there too. This idea is relatively common for Black mothers across the globe. Many Black children grow up knowing that the place where you are disrespectful or disobedient to your parents is the place where you will be chastised. We also often grew up seeing white children have drastically different experiences. Their parents believed in private chastisement. "I'm going to tell your father, Billy." "Wait till we get home, Cindy." But oh baby, my participant-observant experience of Black parental correction has found that a Black mother is not waiting to get you in private to chastise you. Hence the language, "Where you show out is where I show out."

When I was in seminary at Starr King School for the Ministry in Berkeley, California, I worked at the front desk for my work-study job.

As the only cisgender Black woman in full-time high residency at that institution claiming to be dismantling white supremacy as a part of its mission statement, I experienced consistent violence to my person exacerbated by the fact that these people would claim to be my allies. White people from the community and a large majority of my white classmates entered and exited a door through which they had to wait for me to buzz them in and out. The larger majority of them did not acknowledge me until they needed something; then, they saw me. I was invisible otherwise. Their ability to ignore me until my labor was required debunked the myth that respectability will keep me safe if I am quiet, because the violence of being ignored is just as damaging as the violence we fear we might experience from taking up space and being loud.

Dealing with liberal-progressive, well-meaning white people was the worst thing I ever had to pay thousands of dollars of grad school tuition to live through. In this experience, I developed the language of *Where You Show Out Is Where I Show Out: An African American Response to Micro and Macro Aggressions*. Because of the intentional invisibility I was experiencing, alongside the violence of attempting to extract labor from me twenty-seven seconds after ignoring me, I had to sit at that front desk and call out many folks for their violence towards me. I was not willing to "wait until we get home" (private chastisement) or "wait until I tell your father" (solely relying on the people in authority) to address the harm because right in this place where you show out is the exact place where I'm going to show out. If you step to this desk and address me after aggressing me by invisibilizing me, I'm going to tell you about the harm, and then I'll politely pass you the stapler. But right where you show out is where I'm going to show out.

The power of *Where You Show Out Is Where I Show Out: An African American Response to Micro and Macro Aggressions* is that very often when groups of people aggress against people in marginalized identities or bodies, it's very easy for them to do the harmful thing and then go on about their business, leaving the burden of their ignorance and violence on the oppressed. Should that marginalized or harmed person attempt to bring up that aggression later, what do you think happens? "Oh, I didn't mean it like that." "That's not what happened." "I don't know what you're talking about." "I don't remember that moment." It's serving gaslight! Bringing the aggression up later also gives the aggressor power to demand more labor from that person by asking them to relive the aggression during an explanation of what happened and why it was an aggression. Whereas this idea of *where you show out is where I show out* means that if you aggress against me in this moment, this is the moment that I'm going to point out that you are being harmful. Someone aggresses against me and in response, I say, "What you just did was an aggression." They can try to ask the question, "What did I do?" To which I will reply, "It happened twenty-seven seconds ago. Replay it in your mind. Whatever you see yourself doing, whether you think it was right or wrong or nothing at all, THAT is what I'm telling you is an aggression. Go process that in your own time and then find another prayer partner to work it out with because what you're not going to do is try to gaslight me into believing that I didn't just experience the aggression that I experienced."

While *Where You Show Out Is Where I Show Out: An African American Response to Micro and Macro Aggressions* as an ethic will not necessarily keep us from the aggressions of the violence of whiteness, it has absolutely taught me the power of being loud—a message and a lesson that my cousin Latresha Gowdy somehow understood when we were little girls. Ultimately, there is no way to be that will keep us completely safe in an anti-Black society. There is no hair color, no outfit, no countenance, no amount of being quiet that will keep us completely safe. And to contort ourselves to be something that we are not to try and prevent ourselves from a violence that has historically

attacked at any moment, for no reason at all—because white supremacist delusion is not rational—is to be complicit in our own silencing.

To actually experience any form of freedom is to be who we are out
loud. This is not a little self-help pamphlet. But there's something
very powerful in the language of actually being yourself, particularly
as it pertains to the ways that misogynoir targets Black girlhood and
Black womanhood as aggressive, loud, much, and wrong just for
showing up as ourselves. That is to say, "I know that I am viewed a
certain way before I even walk into the room, but I'm still going to
walk into the room as myself. I'm still going to show up as my worthy
self because my worthy self is the place where God gets to shine
through me, as me."

What I have learned is that there is no freedom to be found in an
inauthentic version of myself. There is no safety there. There is no
liberation there. There is no revolution there. MC Breed was right:
"There ain't no future (or freedom) in yo' frontin'."

The freedom to be loud is revolutionary. My cousin, in her red,
yellow, green, and blue hair, her huge smile, her big laugh, her loud
voice in private and in public, saying, "I know y'all want me to be quiet
about this thing that you're doing to me that I do not approve of, but
it ain't gonna happen," is a revolution. Loudness is a worthy contribution to our liberation struggle because if there's one thing a free Black
girl gon' be, it's "too much." And we stan a "too much" Black girl
because a "too much" Black girl today is light-years ahead of the
appropriated, acceptable, white version of her coming to a raggely li'l
runway near you in about twenty-five years.

IN PURSUIT OF

SOFTNESS

"I shall become, I shall become a collector of me.
And put meat on my soul."
—SONIA SANCHEZ

I am popping in Harlem. I've been saying that long before I ever lived in Harlem because every time I would visit the city, I would be walking through the streets, and the sun would be shining on me *especially different*. The men would be complimenting me *especially different*. The energy, the culture, the history would be calling to me *especially different*, and it was just something about who it is that I get to be as my most blackity Black, audacious self, in Harlem, USA.

Living in Harlem did not disappoint me. Whatever it was that I had been dreaming about for years that would happen for me if I could just live in Harlem absolutely happened for me times a trillion by the time I lived there. If it was love that I imagined, your girl got some cute little love. If it was attention from Black men who saw and affirmed all my curves and my unfiltered, natural face and nappy hair . . . check! If it was experiencing the historic energy and legacy of the ancestors and elders who built Harlem brick by brick with their brilliance, I got to wade in that daily—from my walks in Marcus Garvey Park, to my make-out sessions at one a.m. on 132nd and Lenox, to my frequent visits to the jazz museums, to baked fish and attieke on 116th. Giggling on the corner of Ruby Dee Place and Ossie Davis Way, coffee dates on boulevards named for Frederick Douglass and Malcolm X, and easy Saturday morning strolls on streets named for James Baldwin and Langston Hughes; Harlem gave me what it was supposed to have gave.

And Harlem also gave me some stuff I didn't ask for. I lived on a corner that was a block away from a hospital, two blocks from a fire station, and three blocks from a police station. There were sirens violently blaring all day, all night on a consistent basis.

New York City is like this, though. It's called a concrete jungle because everything is concrete. The buildings are brick. The asphalt streets are dark. There are very few trees, and grass is not plentiful. My poor little dog learned to pop a squat in the middle of the road at some point, unable to frolic through lush pastures very often, if at all.

Even the attention that I used to love from the men could often be too much. Being catcalled for an entire block when I'd already smiled brightly at your "Aye, ma, you lookin' too right in them yoga pants" and said all my polite "thank yous" and "no thank yous" and "I got a man's" even though I did not, in fact, have a man, but *I just wanna go to the bodega without having to give you my number today* hard.

I mean hard in the literal sense of walking on pavement, having concrete bedroom walls, and living in brick buildings with the view of more brick buildings. Sometimes the sun shines too brightly on that hard asphalt; other times, the shade from the buildings makes everything gray. And everywhere has stories and stories of floors that you, often, must walk up. It can be debilitating. It can be disabling—and I mean ableist. Take the stairs up or down to the train. Plan out extra time if you will require an elevator or an escalator because your local station's elevator may be out of order, under construction, or just non-existent. The loud noises, the bright lights, the confusing smells. They don't say, "If you can make it in New York City you can make it any-where" for no reason. It is sensory overload, and to survive and thrive, or to simply be well, you gotta put in work.

And even with all of that said, New York is still one of my favorite cities in the entire world. Don't they call that an oxymoron when two things are true at the exact same time? "It was the best of times, it was the worst of times . . ." Was Dickens writing about my time living in New York City? Because, girl.

In late 2019, I saw a video on social media of the NYPD SWAT team surrounding a train car waiting to arrest a young Black man for fare evasion. As everyone else left the train, I watched this young man ask a stranger, "Can someone call my mom?" The police removed everyone from the train, aggressively grabbed this young man up, tossed him onto the disgusting metro-car floor, put his hands behind his back, and handcuffed him—over two dollars and seventy-five cents.

I don't know what happened to him after that video. I just remem-ber feeling so sad about seeing a grown man, sitting in terror, asking for his mother. This was during a time when the NYPD aggressively increased their presence at each train station in an attempt to ramp down fare evasion. Police at each station around Times Square were equipped with machine guns. Police stood on random corners in groups of five and six for the sole purpose of intimidation, looking menacingly at passersby just trying to get some vegan mac and cheese from the local soul food vegan restaurant. This is another way that living in New York was hard. And I mean hard as in violent, forceful, heavy, thick, rigid—as in not easy. But this is also how hard it is to exist, in this body, in America.

I saw the subway arrest video just days before going to London, England, to visit a beautiful Black British man whom I was dating at the time. We will call him Ronald. Ronald was tall, dark, and handsome. And this isn't the ironic tall, dark, and handsome, which usually, confusingly, means a white man with dark hair. I mean literally six foot three, Black like he was born in the sun, and nice thick arms *like I like 'em*. His beard deserves its own paragraph. And that accent coming from that face and body . . . (insert spastic air humping here). He was fine! He was also very kind, gentle-hearted, generous, and thoughtful. And a really good kisser.

* * *

When I was with Ronald, I didn't have to think about anything. He planned everything and thought of everything to the exclusion of nothing. Food, transportation, date nights—I felt so held in that experience that I found myself melting into my seat deeper as each day went by, almost as if I didn't have to get up or stand up for anything.

Time with Ronald, out of the USA, was such a gentle place for me to land in this particularly hard season of my life. One day, I was en route home from a panel I was speaking on a few hours away in Bristol. Ronald and I were supposed to go out for dinner that night. He texted me when I was still an hour or so away from the apartment and asked, "What is your ETA back to London, innit?" (He didn't say "innit," but I just needed to find a way to make him as British as he is.) I replied, "I'm about an hour away, bruv." (Also, I did not call that man "bruv," but again, I'm in character.) He texted back, "I'm a little farther away than you. I'll order food for you, and it'll be there by the time you arrive. We'll figure out the rest of the night when I get there."

I was so impressed with the way that I didn't have to use my brain to think about anything but what I was going to wear for the day when

I was with him. I didn't even have to say, "I'm hungry." That was a given. I also didn't have to say, "I'm too hungry to wait for you to arrive from work to eat." That also was a given. He held so much space for me to just exist that I didn't have to do anything but the work (the panel in Bristol) and the kissing (lots of good kissing) that I came there to do.

It would be easy to say, "Well, sis, you could have had that experience in New York. You are just used to dating trash men." And I wouldn't necessarily negate that into a fistfight, but there were other things that were impacting my ease in that time as well. I was away from the sirens, the stairs, the concrete, the hustle and bustle, the bright lights, the honking horns, and the random "A yooooo" or "Yerrrrr" being yelled outside my window out of nowhere in the middle of the New York City night.

I was also a Black American woman in Europe. Many of our elders and ancestors have similar stories about being both Black and femme in Europe—similar shared experiences and stories about this undefined, often elusive spaciousness that exists for many of us there—to breathe in a way that America just does not give the same space for Black women to just breathe. This whole chapter is about the nervous system. I am sure that Angela Davis, who also spent considerable time in Europe, would have a better language for what the actual reason is that Europe tends to be softer on Black American women's nervous systems. But for me, I like to explain it as, "Those are not my white people." I say that because as a Black American woman and a descendant of chattel slavery, a form most brutal in the southern states of the United States of America, my body has a memory of grief on American soil that it does not have to actively process, in the same way, outside of the United States. Also, in my lived experience, southern Black Americans are the most polite people on the planet, so I contextualize that anywhere I go so I don't mistake a cultural difference for something that it might not be. But, in particular, Europeans do be rude. Rude is very different from racist, though. When I'm experiencing racism in the USA, I know, "This is racism. My bones know this well." When I'm having an experience in Europe, it's so much easier for me to say, "You're being rude. Can I get my gotdamn croissant with some strawberry jam or not? Merci beaucoup, bitch!"

Is the rudeness that I may encounter in Europe okay? Absolutely not. Am I suggesting that white people in Europe are not racist? Hell to the no, no, no. Clearly, those are the direct descendants of the folk who colonized the globe. But the difference between what I experience as rudeness from white people in Europe and what I know is racism from white people in the United States of America is my body's history with white people in the USA. These American white people and I have an intimate relationship with their particular form of racial violence, whereas in Europe, those are not my white people. I am attempting to make it clear that my experience as a Black American woman outside of the USA is a unique semi-privilege that can mostly only be contextualized through shared experience. Ask Mahogany L. Browne and Yazmin Monet Watkins why Paris has their heart. Ask Crystal McCreary why Portugal makes her feel like she can get up off the ground and fly. Ask Khadijah Abdul-Mateen to explain how London changed how she exists in the world, forever. Ask Sonya Renee Taylor about how living in New Zealand radically transformed her spiritual and mental health. Ask Tina Strawn how Jamaica and Costa Rica gave her language for what freedom in her Black femme body really felt like for the first time. I would guarantee that all the Black girls I listed above will tell you that leaving the USA gave us access to an ease and a softness that being in the States rarely affords us. I would wager that all the Black girls I listed would also agree that part of the ease and softness afforded in those experiences has something to do with some version of "those are not my white people."

It also feels important to note that while I was in London, I never saw a police officer with a gun until I went to Buckingham Palace. That was the moment I realized that I had not seen police officers with guns the entire time I was in London, which I learned is because 90 percent of police officers do not carry guns in the UK. The automatic trigger that I normally experience in the USA when I see police officers with guns did not exist for me in London in the same way because, at that point, I had gone a full week without seeing a police officer with a gun.

The tenderness of Ronald taking care of me, the quiet space that I was in away from the harsh noisiness of New York City, the chance to step away from American racism, and the reality that I was in a place where the police did not have guns at their ready use were all contributing to my body having space to crave something that it had no historical concept of embodying—a soft existence. While there, I wrote in my journal:

I want this daily. I do not want to have to go on a retreat to experience this. I want to be able to sit down inside of myself and feel this ease. I do not want to wake up every day feeling anxious. I want to be inside of relationships with beautiful Black men, whom I'm obsessed with, who have the full capacity to hold me and see me as deserving of the kind of generous and thoughtful support that I offer to them daily. What I want is to not be a StrongBlackWoman just because I am a Black woman who happens to be strong. I want a chance to be soft.

SOFT|NESS /'sȯf(t)nəs/:
A state of embodied, full-seated consciousness,
A condition of being wholly relaxed into the mind and body,
The place in which one trusts their own vulnerabilities,

A place where one can trust others with their own
   vulnerabilities,
To be tender and act from that tenderness,
The safe space from which one expects to be handled as if they
   are precious,
An intentional, internalized spaciousness for steady breathing,
An investment in a nervous system that is healing and
   stabilizing from various traumas.

In 2018, I was on a panel that was moderated by image activist Michaela Angela Davis. This feels like a slight flex because Michaela Angela Davis has been so important to Black girlhood and Black womanhood culture for as long as I can remember. Her unapologetic voice, matched with her free-woman fashions and tightly coiled, sandy-blonde Afro that she is well-known for, moves into every room in every space and demands and commands respect and attention. I was sitting up there on that panel nervous AF because, yes, I'm happy to have been invited to the discussion, but also, I'm sitting next to Erika Motherfreakin' Alexander and Thee Michaela Angela Davis. Needless to say, my imposter syndrome had me overthinking every single answer before I spoke.

I kept looking down the table at Michaela, and I couldn't help but think, "Wow. She is such a fully seated woman. She seems so relaxed in her body, as if she trusts that she has no reason whatsoever to speak from any place other than from her fully seated self." She never spoke too loudly. She never stuttered. Her assertions never sounded like questions. We were talking about serious things, yet her tone remained even, her disposition remained tender, and her contributions, all of which were powerful, remained gentle.

That was the deepening of my softness journey.

I wanted to know what it felt like to be able to be in a one-on-one conversation, on a panel, on a dais or a pulpit, on television, a live interview, or even onstage at Essence Fest (hint, hint) and remain fully seated in my body.

My definition of softness is NOT about respectability politics, nor does it see white femininity as an aspiration. This definition is not even thinking about white women other than taking the time to point out white women's easeful access to a form of softness that Black women have historically not had access to. This definition of softness is NOT about a certain appearance. Softness is NOT about widely standardized femininity or the divine feminine archetype. It is not about wealth privilege. It is NOT about money. This definition is NOT about luxury. Softness is NOT about being bougie (especially since Lyvonne Briggs asked y'all to stop calling Black girls bougie because we do not call nonblack girls who like or have nice things bougie). But softness isn't even about having things. Softness is NOT just for the girls. But it's my book, and I am talking to the Black girls. So this is for the Black girls who deserve softness and a society that makes space for their softness.

The opposite of softness is a society that forces Black women to be hard and to only feel safe when being firm, being considered harsh, trusting a lurid disposition, and leaning into the sharpness of life. Having to get up out of the seat of self to respond, protect, and be safe. Being pulled from the seated self to be framed as the aggressor. The opposite of soft is not strong because soft women are strong. But the opposite of soft is the condition of only trusting a hard, unseated strength. The opposite of soft is the world's expectation that we will unseat ourselves to be their expectation of strength and that to say something "powerful," I would have to get out of both my spiritual inner seat and my literal seat to speak.

Toni Morrison is my divine archetype of a soft woman. How many interviews have we watched of her speaking about heavy, hard things—fully seated? After Sister Toni transitioned in 2019, Thea Monyeé and I spent a lot of time talking about whatever that thing is that Toni Morrison had that made it possible for her to exist in that way. It would eventually be named "The Seat of Toni" in later discussions, but when I talk about that "thing," I always describe it as "a soft place from which Toni Morrison, fully seated in herself, stayed ready to tell hard truths while remaining regulated in her nervous system." Think of her interview with Charlie Rose in 1993 where she asks, "If I take your race away, and there you are all strung out, and all you've got is your little self, and what is that? What are you without racism? Are you any good? Are you still strong? Are you still smart? Do you still like yourself? . . . If you can only be tall because somebody's on their knees, then you have a serious problem." Her voice—even. Her body—relaxed. Her face—still. You can't tell me that there aren't PhD levels worth of brilliant lessons to learn in her words, her tone, her body language, and her certainty. That is softness, and that is the proof that softness does not equal weak or not strong.

Nayyirah Waheed wrote, "You do not have to be a fire for every mountain blocking you. You could be a water and soft river your way to freedom too." The idea of being water and soft rivering my way into freedom, versus having to burn everything down in order to get to freedom, honestly never crossed my mind before I walked up on the possibility of a chance to be soft. I have been traumatized and triggered into unseated, harsh, reactionary responses my whole life. What I deserve is to be able to find safety for myself in ways that don't require me to sacrifice my ease, my calm, my sacred seat, or my softness.

Dr. Chanequa Walker-Barnes insinuates a similar question in her book *Too Heavy a Yoke: Black Women and the Burden of Strength* as she teases out the way that we normally describe Black women, starting with the word "strong." She explains how the perpetuation of the "StrongBlackWoman" trope is detrimental to Black women's physical and emotional well-being. Walker-Barnes's book scrutinizes the effects of the expectations that society, the Black church, and families place on Black women to engage in unhealthy, self-sacrificing behaviors while pretending as if the Black woman is not suffering when, in fact, she is suffering. In a 2014 interview, Dr. Walker-Barnes says, "First I noticed it among my therapy clients, many of whom were professional Black women on the verge of physical and emotional breakdown from trying to be strong. Then I noticed it in the church. And when I started looking into health statistics, I realized that there is a major health epidemic among Black women in this country that is hidden under the veneer of strength."

"In Pursuit of Dreaming" introduces Nanny's words from Zora Neale Hurston's *Their Eyes Were Watching God*: "De nigger woman is de mule of de world." It's a world in which society expects Black women to, in humble compliance, perform grim and arduous tasks with superhuman strength. Our families, lovers, and children describe us that way; in fact, they encourage us to be the StrongBlackWoman through their spoken and unspoken expectations of us to hold all things. They also demand this of us due to their own internalized trauma that causes hardness that makes it impossible for them to co-create soft, safe spaces for us to exist and not have to go on retreats or leave the country in order to find. We are even socialized into describing ourselves as strong and wearing that strength as a badge of honor. But, soft Black women, in your lifetime, have you ever even started off describing a Black woman and thought to yourself, "She's so soft"?

And it's not that soft Black women don't exist. It's that Black women very rarely, if ever, get to be safe enough to be soft because softness requires a level of vulnerability that can only come when one feels safe. Because there is no public affirmation of a soft Black woman enough to name it, recognize it, or emulate it, we don't even have full language to ask for it from ourselves and our community. Until now.

My best friend's daughter, Talani, is one of the most vulnerable Black girls I have ever met. I would absolutely describe Talani as free, playful, vulnerable, and soft because whatever Talani wants, needs, is feeling, and is experiencing, the rest of us are clear about it. She is not hiding; it is not a secret. I say "Talani Taught Me" because I am so in awe while watching this young Black girl experience something that I have historically felt like I didn't have access to in this Black femme body. Talani is the kind of teenager who will whimper. Yes, whimper. She will cry. She will squeal. She will whine. She will tell you that she's not having a good day. And then she will have you invested in listening to her Marvin Gaye playlist, lighting incense with her, and offering flowers to her ancestor altar as she sits with them, requesting they come and weep with her too.

Talani has no concept of herself as weak. She is a brilliant leader who is notorious for challenging leadership when she feels unseen or unsafe, but she does it from her soft, seated self. She is so seated, in fact, that you, too, will create space for the moment for her to feel her feelings. There's something so beautiful and sweet about experiencing this type of vulnerability through Talani that even if it is foreign to you, you want to see it, you want to watch it, you want to touch it, and you want to see what's on the other side of it. It makes me wonder who other Black girls and Black women will get to be if we get to create soft realities for ourselves and if we had communities equally invested in co-creating those soft spaces for us to squeal, whimper, cry, whine, be held like babies, and still be seen as serious, worthy, credible, and strong. If "the folk" understood that our softness does not negate our strength whatsoever.

Our journey towards that kind of existence is profound. It is transformative. It is revolutionary. It, too, is our activism.

* * *

Since starting this deep work around softness, I actually ended my public scholarship work on race, which was the larger part of my income. That's how serious it was for me to be in deep integrity with what my body desires and deserves around softness. I was telling this man I was dating that I was ending this work and trying to explain "why" to him. He couldn't understand because he knew that was the bulk of my income, and I was making some really cute money doing the work I was doing. One day I was journaling about it, and these words came to me: "If I keep doing this work, I won't get to be soft." He and I had been on this softness journey together for the past few years, at that point, so when I told him this, he understood, deeply, how important softness had become for me.

I think that may be the case for many of us: "If we keep doing this work this way, we will not get to be soft," and that seems so, so unfair. Not just for us but for future Talanis who need us to understand "softness" in order to create and hold more space for their softness too.

The pursuit of softness is a part of my activism because the dramatic shift that this type of pursuit causes to my nervous system, to stay soft versus immediately going into my triggered and traumatized StrongBlackWoman mode, is getting me closer to tangible freedom that I know I have never held onto before. My softness journey is a radical revolutionary journey. One day you will be describing me, and you will say, "EbonyJanice—she's so soft." I already love that for me.

IN PURSUIT OF
MY BODY

"I'm gonna look for my body. I'll be back like real soon."
—SOLANGE KNOWLES

I'm weary of the ways of the world
Be weary of the ways of the world
I'm weary of the ways of the world
I'm gonna look for my body yeah
I'll be back like real soon
I'm gonna look for my body yeah
I'll be back like real soon
—SOLANGE, "Weary"

The lyrics to Solange Knowles's song "Weary" have arguably been the soundtrack to my Black womanhood journey for the last several years. I am weary of the ways of the world, and I do find that I need to go look for my body on a regular basis. The lyrics make me think about my body being a separate thing from myself and how I've been in pursuit of the ownership of myself for so long. Searching for me feels like the pursuit of freedom. The work of liberation, particularly for Black women, is to be able to go in pursuit of. These are my hands; they are for me. They are not for labor. They are not for someone else's benefit. These are my breasts; they are for me to choose what I do with them—to experience pleasure and whatever other things I decide to do with these breasts, these legs, these thighs—and so, "I'm going to look for my body. I'll be back like real soon." There is so much in the "pursuit of my body" that feels like self-care. It feels like revolution. It feels like righteous indignation. I'm going to look for my body. I will get back to y'all. I will be back to contribute *when I am able*. That is what my life and my mission is right now. My life is an intentional pursuit of my body as something that belongs to me and is for me.

In her essay "Sin, Nature, and Black Women's Bodies," Delores S. Williams explains that there is a "relation between the defilement of earth's body and the defilement of Black women's bodies" (*Ecofeminism and the Sacred*, ed. Carol J. Adams, New York: Continuum, 2007: 24). She argues that the logic of domination, patriarchy, and a culture of violence against the feminine systematically "beat down" on the bodies, souls, and minds of Black women and upon the earth.

Delores S. Williams names the systematic oppression of Black women and the earth as sin. Womanist ethics professor Melanie L. Harris offers that by using theological language, Williams is highlighting the moral stakes of environmental racism and accentuates the religious significance of the justice concerns of Black women. Drawing a parallel between strip-mining and the constant rape and sexual violence enacted upon the bodies of enslaved Black women, Williams asserts that the sin of defilement "manifests itself in human attacks upon creation so as to ravish, violate, and destroy creation, to exploit and control the production and reproduction capacities of nature, to destroy the unity in nature's placements, to obliterate the spirit of the created" (*Ecofeminism and the Sacred*, ed. Carol J. Adams, New York: Continuum, 2007: 25). Basically, what she's saying is that

Black women's bodies are the only bodies that have historically been used for both labor and reproduction.

But my freedom starts with me, and in this form, at some point, this vessel that carries my whole spirit and soul is all I have. Freedom starts with this body then. At the very least, if this body is my own, then that gives me a starting point through which to even create anything else, to contribute anything else; at the very least, this body has to be mine. At which point, Black girls and women decide, no, this body is not just for labor, not just for someone else's pleasure, not just for reproduction, not for the world to glean and benefit from in ways that Black women don't get to benefit in our bodies. That is the beginning of powerful revolution.

As a hip-hop womanist, of course I look to the work of hip-hop and third-wave feminist and womanist scholars, such as Joan Morgan and Tamura Lomax, who have been writing about the reclamation of Black women's bodies both inside of hip-hop culture and from hip-hop culture for years. So, again, this is not an assertion that Black feminists and womanists have not been reclaiming the Black feminine form and subverting both the white and patriarchal gaze as it pertains to our autonomy since the beginning of time. A fourth-wave womanist reclamation has new platforms through which we go to look for our bodies—a theory we have the privilege to both discuss and put into radical public practice as a result of the Black women folk before us.

I can think about my own relationship with my body and how I can feel very disconnected from the way I look as a result of body dysmorphic disorder, which I experience as an extremely deep insecurity around being as shapely as I naturally am. Society critiques the meaning of my thighs and tries to tell me what my hips mean, what these curves mean. Isn't it ironic that the world can benefit from my body by taking a picture of this shapeliness to a doctor and saying, "Give me this body type," while I sit over here and suffer from body dysmorphic disorder? My body *type* has become the standard but not the actual natural form of shapeliness that I exist in. So I have to process that even while loving my body, it doesn't get to belong to me. This isn't a judgment of plastic surgery—this is to suggest that someone should not be able to manufacture a version of my body and be celebrated for it while I, in this natural form, have my body critiqued as "too much," "fat," "overweight," "unhealthy," and "wrong."

A major part of my freedom work is to decide that it doesn't matter what anybody else is doing outside of this body. Me, EbonyJanice, the person who is manifested in this form, is a free woman. This belongs to me. This is mine. This body was given to me for my great pleasure, not to this world for its critique, for its demand, or for its expectations and consumption. It is mine to choose what to do with, and the intentional pursuit of that power within myself says that if I did nothing else, that in itself is revolutionary; that in itself is my activism; that in itself is freedom work.

"I'll be back like real soon."
—SOLANGE

The lyric that comes right before "I'm gonna look for my body (yeah); I'll be back like real soon," that she repeats over and over again is, "I'm weary of the ways of the world." To be in the body and in constant pursuit of the body is a weary-making reality. She is saying, "This is heavy. Carrying the weight of burdens and expectations of the world on my back and shoulders is too much. I've been carrying these expectations like a huge water pail on my head. And I see how that does not benefit me at all. It looks like it benefits the folk. It looks like it benefits the community. It looks like it benefits the world. But not me." It doesn't benefit me. Therefore, it doesn't actually benefit everybody else.

"You're not getting the highest version of me; I'm tired. You're not getting the highest version of me; I'm weary. You're not getting the highest version of me; I feel 'buked and scorned. So let me just put you all on notice that I'm going to look for my body. I'm going to look for my ease. I'm going to look for a way to lay these burdens down for real. I'm going to look for a place where I can rest. I'm going to look for a place where I am actually sovereign." Sometimes that is a literal "I'm leaving this place physically." And sometimes that's just deciding that whatever we were doing, we're not doing that anymore. Not like this. So when I say, "I'll be back like real soon," I'm saying that once I have found my body, I'll return as a more whole version of myself, able to resume this relationship as a more whole version of myself. But not a moment sooner. And I'm taking obvious liberties with my own understanding of this song, but this is the way that it impacts me: "I might not ever come back after I have relocated myself." That may be physically and/or my return is with a boundary, and the boundary means that this relationship and the way we existed before this time doesn't exist anymore. "I'm going to look for my body. I'll be back like real soon" is radical and revolutionary because, historically, Black women have not had permission to decide to create those kinds of boundaries. "When I get back from finding my body and my glory, things are going to be different." That decision is going to change everything. That decision has already started to change things.

Angela Davis writes about the mamification of Black women in her essay "Reflections on the Black Woman's Role in the Community of Slaves." She really breaks this down, allowing us to understand the origins and the creation story of Black women's bodies for something and someone else other than labor and other than for "the folk." She offers that the way history tells the story of Black womanhood has decided that because we are the so-called mothers of all creation, that means we are now expected to "mother" all things. We have to nurse.

We have to soothe. We have to fix. We have to absolve. We have to carry everything. Davis's essay breaks down how the mamification of Black women still serves towards the socialization of Black women as "mothers," and the mothers are expected to hold and carry all things. Therefore, at which point, *de nigger woman* decides, "I'm not holding or carrying all of that anymore," the world is like, "What?" The systems are like, "What?" Our communities are like, "What?" Oftentimes, even we are like, "What?"

An article from 1918 in the *Greenville News* of Greenville, South Carolina, entitled, "Negro Women to Be Put to Work," says, "City Ordinance Soon Be Passed Requiring Them to Be Regularly Employed." This newspaper clipping goes on to say, "Regardless of whether they want to or have to, able-bodied negro women in Greenville who are not regularly employed are to be put to work, put in jail, or fined heavily." Further, "It was decided that an ordinance, similar to the one now in force requiring all able-bodied men to work at least five days per week, should be passed with regard to these women." *These women*, not *all women*. It continues, "A number of complaints have come to members of Council of negro women who are not at work and who refuse employment when it is offered them, the result being that it is exceedingly difficult for families who need cooks and laundresses to get them. Wives of colored soldiers, getting a monthly allowance from the Government, have, a number of them, declined to work on the ground that they can get along without working, according to reports. Others have flatly refused jobs without giving any reason whatsoever, while still others pretend that they are employed when, as a matter of fact, they derive a living from illegitimate means. The proposed ordinance will require them all to carry a labor identification card showing that they are regularly and usefully employed, and the labor inspectors and police will be charged with the duty of rigidly enforcing the law."

So the Black woman was taking the time at night to press her clothes and set her hair in rollers. She was living in her residence, cooking, cleaning, decorating, feeding, washing, clothing, and grooming her own babies. She was worried about her husband and writing him love letters to keep his spirits high while he was at war. Then white people decided they were too lazy to cook for themselves and wash the filth off their own clothes. These white people created and enforced laws that required Black women to work in white homes, and then Black women had to go home, late at night, and give whatever was left over to their own, all while many able-bodied white women did nothing. So the Negro woman had decided, "I'm not working." "I'm not laboring." "I'm not producing anything else." "I'm going to go look for my body. I'll be back like real soon," and the world said, "Girl? What? Never! That's illegal!"

When my little cousin was about six years old, I saw her walk through a living room full of family members, mostly men. She started pulling at her shirt to cover her butt. And I noticed that because I had very similar experiences growing up where I was constantly trying to make sure that, even as a little girl, something was covering my butt if I had on leggings or pants where the shapeliness of my behind was showing. It triggered me to see this little cousin having this experience because it made me think about how often the family would be like, "Britney got a big old butt! Look at Britney. Come here, Big Booty Britney," making various jokes about her booty. And I grew up with jokes like that well into my adulthood. But particularly, I remember as a teenager and in my early twenties being called *Big Booty Judy* or having some other joke told about my butt by family members. What I noted in my little cousin already knowing that her body was a thing she should feel some kind of way about, is that our familial decision to talk publicly about her body was just yet another way that we were taking away her autonomy—the same way that my own autonomy over my body was taken away from me when I was her age.

Some of the ways we take away body autonomy from little Black girls, which supports us growing into Black women who struggle with seeing and loving our bodies, is by using language like "fast (or fass) tail little girl." For my little cousin Britney, age six, to be walking through a room full of boys and men, all of whom she is absolutely safe with yet she somehow knows that she should be trying to cover her butt as she walks through the room with them, suggests that she's already learned that she should have some shame around her body. She has already internalized that she should do something above and beyond to cover this part of herself that she was just born with naturally, which would indicate that her body is wrong.

One of the ways in which I learned the same behavior as a little girl is with language like, "Go somewhere and sit ya little fast tail down, walking back and forth through this room." Just the action of walking through the room suggested that I was intentionally doing something to entice whoever was in the room, whether it was the boy cousins or some other grown man. Therefore, the responsibility of my own modesty was put in my little four-, five-, six-year-old hands; even the responsibility of protecting myself was put in my young, little, adolescent hands.

* * *

Did my guy cousins have anybody telling them to cover themselves? No. When I was growing up, sitting in the front row of church after Sunday school with my cousin Rommel to the left and our childhood friend Curtis to the right, did either of them have to put something over their legs to cover them? No. Even if I had on pants that fit the form of my body, I needed to cover up my legs. There is no way to make it make sense that the three of us could be sitting right there next to each other, yet I'm the only one expected to cover even though we all have on pants. My own participant observation and anthropological research (my expert lived experience) shows that very same experience in other public places. There is nobody else asked to be as modest as Black women and girls.

In the fall of 2016, a young teacher in Atlanta, Georgia, was ridiculed and criticized for being too sexy for her elementary school students. They came up with the hashtag #teacherbae to reference her. #Teacherbae in and of itself sexualizes who she is, not that she is just the teacher but that she is the sexy teacher, that she is Teacher Bae. Does she do something sexual in these photos that she's posted of herself on social media? No. Is she saying anything sexual or flirtatious in these photos that she's posted of herself on social media? Absolutely not. But because you can see the shapeliness of her body, there is a conversation in the comment section across several platforms that she is dressed inappropriately and that she is doing something wrong. Because I have experienced this critique of my own body growing up, both in church and in professional spaces, when this happened I decided to try to find photos of white women in very similar dresses or outfits to what this young lady had on in the photos. I found a photo of a slim white woman wearing a similar dress as the Black teacher. I put those two photos side by side, then shared it on my own social media. It was evidence that the Black teacher was not being critiqued because she was dressed wrong; she was being critiqued because the world sees her body as wrong. When these two women wear the same exact thing, one is seen as professional, and the other is not.

Another such example is when you see Black girls in public with shapely butts, hips, and thighs with short shorts on. You don't even call those shorts. There is something socialized into you, if you are particularly from this culture, to automatically call those "booty shorts," "Daisy Dukes," or even "coochie cutters." Yet when a white woman with slim legs rocks short shorts, even if your own modest proclivities call you to identify them as short, there is a drastically different judgment just in the name that you call them. "I saw this Black girl today with a big booty with some coochie cutters on" versus "I saw this girl today at the mall with some short shorts on." That language by itself is indicative of what it is that you're saying about the body of the person. Same shorts, same dress, same skirt—different reaction. So it is not the actual clothes that are inappropriate. It is the body that is being deemed inappropriate.

This, of course, makes me think of Sarah Baartman. Baartman was a South African enslaved woman with a condition called steatopygia, which results in protruding of flesh and fat in the butt. She was sold to the circus and lived out the last years of her life as a circus attraction just for people to show up and look at her butt. After she died, her brain, skeleton, and sexual organs remained on display in a Paris museum until 1974. Her remains weren't repatriated and buried until 2002. She died in 1815. I said, an African woman's butt was on display in a museum in Europe until the year of our Lord, two thousand and two. It is alarming that the dehumanization of the Black feminine form is neither experienced as human nor is it allowed to belong to the self.

From a very young age, my Black feminine body is sexualized. It is critiqued. It is stolen. It is fetishized. It is picked apart. It is never my own. It can often feel impossible for us to escape this story and loss of our bodies. These stories come from home, the Black family, the church, the education system, the healthcare industry, and even the way we are perpetuated in art. Black women's body ownership is a justice issue. One such obvious proof is the maternal Black health crisis. Black women are three times more likely to die from a pregnancy-related cause than white women. Multiple factors contribute to these disparities, such as variation in quality healthcare, underlying chronic conditions, structural racism, and implicit bias.

Black women's bodies are a political site, but we deserve our bodies to simply be sites of liberation. The fact that policies such as The

CROWN Act, which is a bill that prohibits discrimination based on a person's hair texture or hairstyle if that style or texture is commonly associated with a particular race or national origin, was passed in 2022 demonstrates the politicization of the feminine Black form.

When I talk in my regular voice, which is a natural alto and often a slightly heavier timbre than a lot of women with higher-pitched voices than my own, the timbre of my voice is often judged as "angry" because it is easy to fall into the lazy trope of calling Black women angry when really I just naturally sound like Peter Brady going through puberty. That I cannot even sound like myself without scrutiny is a justice issue.

The work that Black women have to do simply to maneuver in basic spaces such as our homes, our churches, our schools, and our jobs is a justice issue because there is no space in which we can actually show up as our whole selves and not have to consider how our bodies will be received.

Anti-Black, patriarchal, white supremacist society intentionally creates the story and the juxtaposition between what is worthy of protection and what is seen as virtuous. It determines who gets to experience protection and who has to fend for themselves because their bodies are inherently considered stronger and able to endure more pain and are essentially less worthy of consideration. Sojourner Truth asked the question, "Ain't I a woman?" when Black men were about to get their right to vote and white women decided that now it was time for a suffrage movement on behalf of their own issues. This was Sojourner Truth's case for intersectionality in 1851 before Kimberlé Crenshaw coined that term in 1989. My contemporary translation of that speech goes something like this:

So, Black men, y'all just gonna pretend like you don't see me over here? We weren't doing different work in the field. So how do you decide that my rights to access this liberty should come after yours when there was not a special Black women's slavery work? And to white women, no one has ever treated me gentile, helped me up into a carriage, or thrown a piece of fabric over a puddle for me to walk over. Do either of you see that my body is worthy of whatever gentleness white women have received as well? And that the very unique experience that I had as a laborer in these fields is especially unique because there was no maternity leave? There was no time between birthing babies and going back to the field or to my work in the home? Am I a woman? Do you see me at all?

If whiteness historically offers white women some protection, and patriarchy has offered Black men some form of power, it's high time for Black women to take a break to go look for our bodies. It's high time for Black women to affirm, "My freedom will be in this body, which was made whole for me. This I'll do in remembrance of myself." This is a radical revolutionary act, and it benefits the whole community when we get to show up as our whole selves.

"I don't want to come across as angry," while holding your breath keeps your face from seeming too hard.

"I don't want to be accused of raising my voice," while lightening your tone to not sound belligerent.

"I don't want to cuss this person out even though they deserve to get told off," while biting your tongue to keep from speaking up.

"I don't want to start crying in this meeting," while tightly pursing the lips into a fake smile.

Or:

Someone says something that hurts you, so you leave the good mood that you were in and rip them into shreds, unable to return to the mood you were in before that moment.

Someone aggresses against you in public and triggers you in an embarrassing way, so you take your hands and lay them on that individual.

Someone calls you a "Black bitch" (not to be confused with a regular "bitch"), and you snap and raise your voice until your throat is hoarse and your body temperature has risen.

There are so many ways that this society triggers us into leaving our bodies, and after years, even generations, of our bodies doing all they can to protect us in various ways from these aggressions, it is likely that many of us are unaware of how infrequently we are actually sitting inside ourselves.

In 2020, when 95 percent of the people in my Harlem apartment building started working from home because of the global health crisis, my anxiety increased on a whole new level. Living in the hood is incredible on most days. You get to live around people who find joy in situations where joy was not being served on the main menu. The conditions can sometimes be unlivable due to the negligence of the local government as it pertains to enforcing building regulations and policies (that actually protect people and ensure we have equal access to other functions our local government is supposed to afford us). Yet, in spite of the ways people in the hood are mishandled, erased, and ignored, one thing folk in marginalized communities and identities are going to do is find some joy.

When our government failed us by not ensuring a proper shutdown in March of 2020, millions of people who had no clue how to work from home were suddenly working from home. This meant that my downstairs neighbors thought playing Afro beats on the highest volume at 9:35 a.m. Eastern Standard Time, at the exact time that I taught my Women in Hip-Hop & Social Change course online on Tuesdays and Thursdays with paper-thin tenement building walls, was a way to find joy in a chaotic situation.

It's effortless to be a mindfulness guru in perfect conditions. But to practice intentional breathing in the hood can be a whole different beast. From the constant sirens of the hospital one block away, the fire station two blocks north, and the police station three blocks east to the children with no playground nearby having to create a play area on the stoop right outside my window at ten a.m. To the loud dance party happening for hours in apartment 3B. To the music blasting in car stereos on the corner once the weather started getting nicer and folk were tired of sitting in the house waiting to hear if we were all really as doomed as we felt. How much "mindfulness" can you practice when life is happening at such a high volume and pace?

There were so many times when I wanted to completely leave my body because of the tight knot in my belly and the lump in my throat. Hell, I wanted to leave the whole city, not just my body. But that is not the reality for all people, so what does "going to go look for my body" look like for the Black girl in conditions where "breath" might not even be a conversation being had?

When I first started intentionally pursuing my wellness journey, yoga was an important practice. Once, while in the pose called downward dog, the yoga instructor bent over beside me and said, "You have to breathe," and that is when I realized that I had been walking around holding my breath. That's not a metaphor for something. Not only was I holding my breath in downward dog, I realized that I had also been walking around holding my breath, in various scenarios, for years. You know why? Because leaving my body (by way of holding my breath) had become a powerful defense mechanism against a traumatizing society.

Reclaiming the breath is reclaiming the body. Any mindfulness education will teach you that to be present with your breath is to actually be present at the moment. And if you use holding your breath as a way to escape pain and violence, how many moments have you missed out on? The literal return to the breath is a major key for our survival. So many of us have been walking around holding our breath because of fear, because of shame, because of guilt, because of condemnation, because of the weight of judgment, or because we are trying to avoid the critique of our body (sucking in your stomach is a form of holding your breath), our voice, and our response was wrong. We are holding our breath because if we even let out a little bit of a sigh, we know that sound will likely be critiqued as anger. How have the many years of depriving the body from breath impacted us physically, emotionally, and spiritually?

Breathing through everything could be the most accessible and free way for us to pursue our bodies. When I returned to my breath, I started to notice that in the moments when aggressions were happening to me, I would be holding my breath, the exchange would pass, and nobody would be corrected. When I started breathing, taking a deep inhale and exhaling that grief and fear off my chest, I was finally able to open my mouth for the first time and say something, even if it was just a simple, "I don't like that." When I began to return to my breathing, I was able to sit in the experience of 2020 and not completely lose myself in all of the noise. Breath gave me a clear head to figure out what to do about the house party under me, and breath gave me the chance to invite my students into their own mindfulness practice during our classes when the background noise of the sirens or even when Wizkid and Burna Boy got louder than we expected. Learning to breathe helps us stay with our bodies and unlearn the ways we leave our bodies to try to cope.

I was thirty-one years old when I realized that my body didn't belong to me. It was the night of my birthday. I was dancing and undressing in the mirror, listening to Beyoncé's "Drunk in Love," which had just come out a month earlier. I got to the part of the song where she sings, "No complaints from my body so fluorescent under these lights," and it hit me that I absolutely had complaints with my body. The more I began to analyze that over the coming weeks, I just kept asking the question, "Are these my complaints? And if they're not, whose complaints are they?" And I heard the voice in the language of the complaint, and that was not my voice.

My body, historically, has been dictated to, governed by, and critiqued mostly by external sources. My body belonged to the church. My body belonged to my family. My body belonged to society. My body belonged to past lovers. My body was not ever my own, and I wondered, especially as a woman who had been using the hashtag #freegirl for years before it was even a hashtag or claiming "je suis une fille libre" since I was a teenager, how didn't I know that the voices that were dictating the way that I moved around in the world in this form were not my own voice?

So I think back to my little cousin, somehow inherently knowing that she needs to maneuver her body at this young age, and I know factually, nobody ever specifically told her, *This is what you should do with your body.* But well before the age of six, she had already been socialized into believing that her body was not good, nor was it her own. Me too. I've been tugging my own proverbial shirt over my butt since I was four or five years old. Just this knowing and just this possibility of having no complaints with my body, seeing it as "so fluorescent under these lights," was the catalyst for a freedom journey that I am worthy of and that all my little cousins deserve. I'm going to go look for my body. I might be back but only if I am safe to return as my own. And that's the work of freedom I'm committed to, both for me and all the Black girls who should get to live in their bodies with ease without having to go in pursuit of the body that was given to each of us as a precious gift.

IN PURSUIT OF
UNASHAMEDNESS

"You cannot police me, so get off my areola."
—JANELLE MONAE

There were two ways that I had to consider writing this chapter. First was a very watered down version that asked for permission to talk about sex. I have been approaching this topic in that voice for twenty-plus years. Then there is this version that you are getting, where I start the chapter by ripping the Band-Aid off of shame and saying, "Your elders have sucked a dick or two or licked a coochie or two or both. The only way we are going to heal shame is to come from behind the idea that they didn't like giving or receiving the orals and the penetrations too; then we'll be able to get to the true truth."

M'kay? Now that we got that out there, let's begin.

Much of my disconnection from my own identity as a Black woman, in this Black feminine form, has been shame around sex and sensuality as taught to me by the Black church. It feels very important to note that there is a unique experience that bapti-costal-cogic girls grew up in that is different from many of our Black girlfriends who were not socialized as intentionally in the strictness of Black church culture. For example, I have a girlfriend who was never told she was going to hell when she was a child. When I learned this, I said, "Oh, baby. We are not the same kind of Black girl." Black girls who grew up with the threat of hell—we are our own genre. This, in itself, proves that Blackness is not a monolith; however, because of the Great Migration, most Black American people across the country have southern roots. As a result, a large percentage of Black women in America have been raised in communal traditions that are largely inspired by the Southern Black Christian experience. Because of that, I know we can all, by and large, relate to many of the themes in this particular chapter—namely, shame.

Years ago in therapy, I found that I would often say, "I don't want to bring shame to my family," and my therapist would be like, "If I had a dollar for every time you say that in therapy, I would be a very wealthy woman." The language of "bringing shame to my family" is intimately related to shame around sexuality and sensuality. A large portion of my young adult years was spent believing that the worst thing I could do is "bring shame to my family" by getting pregnant before I was married. Or everybody finding out that I'm kind of a nasty freak. Think about that. I believed that riding reverse cowgirl, throwing that thing in a circle unmarried, and enjoying it was the worst thing I could do. Really?

I can think of more shameful activities. However, based on my upbringing, this is the terror that was socialized into me. I didn't understand those natural desires, actions, and behaviors until I was an adult with new language around bliss and pleasure in the body. Therapy helped me name that it was the fear of shaming my family that was keeping me from authenticity in several areas of my life. I grew up believing the language of "urges," of "denying the flesh," and "the body being inherently sinful." And so there was no connection between my body and my desire for pleasure. The available language of "giving in to an urge" and "experiencing pleasure" were two drastically different things, and there was no relationship or connection for me. As that version of myself—the one who was afraid of bringing shame to my family—I couldn't understand that pleasure isn't inherently or exclusively bad or sinful. Pleasure is a basic, natural desire most animals experience as a part of their being.

A major part of our freedom journey must be to deconstruct, question, and contextualize our irrational fears of bringing shame to our family by experiencing sexual pleasure or acknowledging our bodies as something worthy of pleasure.

If I could tell my younger self anything, it would be, number one, take better care of your teeth because Cardi B wasn't lying when she said it took a bag to fix her teeth, so she hope you hoes know it ain't cheap. Trust me. It ain't. And dental insurance is a scam and an elusive privilege. Number two, I would tell younger EbonyJanice to have more *guilt-free* sex. I wasted so much time feeling guilty about sex that I don't even know if I ever enjoyed the fullness of it. Guilt was sitting right there at the end of that orgasm looking at me like, "Hey, nasty girl, with yo nasty self." I missed it. If I still acknowledged sex outside of marriage as sin, I would say that was a wasted sin. I should have enjoyed it at the very least. Not even that I should have had more sex, just more sex without the guilt, shame, and condemnation that I experienced when it was over.

I had been thinking, a lot, about my unintentional celibacy and the residual guilt and shame that I was lingering in about desiring sex while unmarried. So I sent a group text to the source of most of my anxiety: my aunts and my mother. I had recently turned thirty-four years old, and I had been celibate for years. I remember my age, specifically, because I thought, "Welp! I've outlived the timeline of Christ.

And if Jesus was allegedly celibate when he went to Calvary at thirty-three, he can now no longer understand my plight at thirty-four."

I texted them because I wondered if they ever thought about me and how I was existing as a single woman without companionship, physical touch, or intimacy. I think a part of me wanted to know if they were even willing to reconsider some of their previous positions on sex and the natural desires of the body. Out of the six of them, one replied and said, "I'm praying for you, baby." She never said what she was praying for, but I would bet large amounts of money that she was not praying that I got some good D soon. My mother replied with words akin to "Ewwww." God bless my mother. Three of them didn't reply at all. One of them called and had a real, game-changing womanist conversation.

Let me explain why this was a womanist conversation. In Alice Walker's definition of womanism, a daughter says to her mother, "Mama, I'm walking to Canada and I'm taking you and a bunch of other slaves with me." Reply: "It wouldn't be the first time." What's happening in this portion of the definition of womanism is intergenerational affirmation and confirmation in the sharing of wisdom and stories that are inherently familial, healing, transformative, and essential to the freedom and liberation journey of all beings in this bloodline. This means that if the daughter never says to the mother, "I'm about to do this 'revolutionary' thing," she might not find out that she's not the first person in her family to do this revolutionary thing. Learning that she is amongst a group of revolutionary people contributes to her ability to take the family from this place in freedom to the next place in freedom. She is finding out that it is her responsibility to take the family higher and to heal them forward. The elders have sacrificed so much to get her to this point. She is now responsible for doing the work to get the next generation to the next place in freedom. Conversely, the mother then is doing her daughter a great service by saying, "You wouldn't be the first," because now it opens the door to have more deep conversation around what other practices have already been successful and which haven't. This intergenerational dialogue gives them the opportunity to talk about where this line of freedom stopped for past generations and where their journey towards freedom is going for future generations.

In the conversation with my aunt I asked, "What do I do at this point? I am living inside of a container of fear that I may bring shame to my family if it is found out that I am pursuing the satisfaction of these sensations and desires. Especially because there is no one in this group text who can fully relate because you all were married with all of your children by this age."

My aunt shared some of her personal stories, and I was blown away to experience her transparency on this topic. It was a very liberating discussion that offered language to reflect on how far this conversation around sex, sensuality, and experiencing pleasure in the body had come through our family for generations. Our conversation helped me to gain clarity about what my responsibility and contribution to that conversation could be for the family and the community of Black women in the future. Some of my role is to simply have the conversation and not just leave those behind me on "read" in the text thread. Some of my role is to also be clear about what I'm praying for when I reply, "I'm praying for you, baby!" Largely, I see my role as telling the truth about my journey and offering another language that replaces the shame that women in our family have felt around this issue for years. Additionally, I see my role as teaching those behind me that it is not wise to allow our own definition of freedom to be formed by people who are not free themselves.

At thirty-four, I had made it the longest in my family, still unmarried, single, with no children. None of my elders made it into their thirties without being married, so they had no real context for what they would be doing in my shoes. This means that I had arrived at a point in my relationship with the elders where they could not guide me with actual lived experience. I know that my specific lived experience matters and is credible because God has not forgotten my circumstance, so there must be wisdom somewhere in the text or in the testimony of the living to support me on this journey.

The conversation, then, of "Mama, I'm walking to Canada and I'm taking you and several other slaves with me," and the mother's response being, "It wouldn't be the first time," happened inside this conversation with my aunt. I was on that call expressing my need to openly pursue and experience sexual pleasure and satisfaction, even if I am not married. I also wanted my aunt to know that I would be taking "several other slaves with me," meaning, I'm not going to let the generations behind me exist in the same kind of shame that I have to this point. Auntie responded, "You wouldn't be the first." You might be the first at this age, but you are not the first person in this bloodline, in this family, or the first Black believer woman who is considering what to do at this point as a non-married woman with this body, in this experience, and on this journey seeking pleasure.

If we're talking about Black women and liberation, we have to talk about Black women and pleasure. It would be insufficient to unpack the pursuit of softness, dreaming, my body, and wellness and not acknowledge that pleasure in this body is a major site of liberation. Remember when we discussed the hypersexualization of Black women in "Pursuit of My Body"? Which is it? Are we hypersexual? Or are we prohibited from experiencing pleasure without fear of bringing shame to our family? It can't be both. We can't be both hypersexual and sexually repressed. Especially not in the United States of America in the lineage of Southern Black Christianity where sex outside of marriage is a sin, and the belief intentionally represses Black girls and women in ways that no other group of people experiences shame.

When my mother got pregnant as a teenager with my oldest sister, she had to stand up and apologize in front of the church. My sister's father was nowhere to be seen for an apology, and that was not uncommon. If you are a Black woman of a certain age growing up in the Southern Black Christian experience, you have either seen or participated in that type of public shaming. So it can't be both. We can't be hypersexual and exist inside of a tradition that makes us apologize when the proof of that experience is revealed.

The pursuit of unashamedness is a part of this liberation journey. Unashamedness is on the other side of our fear of judgment, of bringing shame to the family, of bringing shame to ourselves, and of bringing shame to the house of the Lord, which is thick in our socialization as Black girls and Black women. Whether you still practice this Christian tradition or not, it is a major tool in our socialization. Therefore, this pursuit of unashamedness is a way to say, "When I am unashamed, I will be closer to freedom than I've ever been, particularly when I am unashamed of this natural experience that's occurring in my body. Then I will be closer to freedom than I've ever been."

The "Pursuit of Unashamedness" is not me writing a whole dissertation saying go have sex any which-a-way, even though it's "your body, your story." What this pursuit of unashamedness is really about is giving us language to, at the very least, ask some questions for ourselves about the socialization, tradition, and upbringing of our youth and what it did not give us access to. So if I would have, at the very least, had that language and been able to ask myself those questions, quite possibly, all of that guilt and shame and condemnation that I've lived with, in my body, wouldn't have impacted my disconnection from my own sensuality and pleasure for so many years.

I remember hearing Pearl Cleage speak at a book festival in Decatur, Georgia, years ago. Someone asked her how she writes through her writer's block. She said, "Usually I write a letter to whomever it is that is keeping me from being able to tell the truth." For me, that person used to be my grandmother, before she transitioned into eternity. Now, it is pretty much an amalgamation of all six of her daughters (my mother and my aunts) . . . and maybe a few other people whom I haven't given a name to yet as I process this, ongoing.

Neither my mother, my aunts, nor my grandmother ever said, "Girrrrrl, you can't be over here telling the truth." But something inside of me is like, "Yo. My family doesn't want the world to know these things about me. Hell . . . THEY don't want to know these things about me." Nevertheless, I felt very committed to telling and being the truth, so inspired by Pearl, I decided to write a fifteen-page letter, which I did not enclose with a kiss, to the womenfolk in my family. That long, rambling, messy mess of a letter supported me in finding the language that I needed to open up a bit about sensuality, my belief in the necessity of the erotic, and the violence of how the Black church had historically kept me from viewing my own holy body as the body of Christ—the literal Black church.

I won't share the whole letter here, but it started like this:

Dear Mama 'nem,
I'm a freak.

I honestly don't know why these folk continue to fool with me when I act like this in real life, but a basic outline of major points I made in that letter are:

1. The fear of our sensuality stems from religious ideology that teaches us some really unrealistic truths about our bodies and their purpose.
2. God designed the clitoris with all those nerves there for a reason. To insist that responding to our body's

natural proclivities is wrong is unfair and contradicts biology.

3. The fear of our bodies feeling something "other than the holy ghost" has plagued the Black Christian community since forever, but who told us it was wrong to feel good?

4. Context matters. CONTEXT: CON·TEXT /ˈkän-tekst/ Noun: the circumstances that form the setting for an event, statement, or idea and in terms of which it can be fully understood and assessed.

5. The condemnation that we come under, especially as Black women, has been historically constructed as a means of control and degradation.

6. Your body is a space of healing and wholeness. So why would you continue to deny portions of yourself that are in want?

7. My body is not a site of sin. My body is a site of liberation. It was molded and shaped by God to be the vessel through which I pursue my divine purpose of proving God in this form and expression. To continue critiquing its natural proclivities as wrong is to question the divine construction of my members as a mistake.

8. Queer theologian Xan West asks: "Who does it benefit for me to believe it this way?"

9. In many instances, bell hooks says, the fascination and subsequent fear of Black sexuality is just another example of the ways that the bodies of Black folk are used to serve the interest of the system that has no intentions of fostering or promoting the growth or freedom of those people.

10. A major reason for your preachment against pleasure is because you were taught not to pursue pleasure. Let's keep it real though, bruh! Your Sunday school teachers didn't

have twelve children and two different baby daddies by accident. They, too, were doing the booty. And many of them were enjoying it with reckless abandon. So whaaaaat is all this shaming we keep on doing of one another for? From generation to generation.

Yes, I really did cut up in that letter like that. How do you think I wrote a fifteen-page letter, typed in twelve-point Times New Roman font? I filled that letter to the brim with everything I was thinking but felt too afraid to say out loud.

I want every one of us to employ this practice, even if you don't share the letter with the ones you write it to. Consider who is in the way of you telling and being the truth, and write a stream of consciousness letter to them to clear the way for your own true words to surface. Those words, whether you say them out loud or not, will support you on your liberation journey because you'll finally have language that is in your voice, and you'll be more equipped to tell the difference between your actual shame and shame that came from your socialization.

In 2019, I remember saying to my therapist, "I want to be myself more than I want anything else in the world." To deny this portion of myself is to negate that deep desire for authenticity. It's impossible for me to actually be the most authentic EbonyJanice without acknowledging these natural desires that I have in my body as worthy of being satisfied. That's the journey now. The entire purpose and point of this season of my life and a major part of my preachment, public teaching, and sharing is that everything about me is good, that who I am is good, and I don't have to equate my body or my desires as inherently sinful or wrong. That's why surrendering shame is revolutionary because everything in this society wants me to hate, reject, and resist myself. So any decision to do exactly the opposite of my actual mission and purpose in this life is radical, transformative, revolutionary, and it is essential to my journey to freedom. It is essential to my intention to heal my ancestors in this journey to freedom, and it is essential to ensuring that the generation to come never has to find out, after the fact, that they wouldn't be the first to do something like that.

IN PURSUIT OF
WELLNESS

"It's okay. You can keep your magic to yourself; keep it tucked away.
They'll have to find another wonder for today. You don't always
have to be the one to save the world. It's okay, girl."
—TASHA, "Lullaby"

I grew up with my paternal grandmother, Bernice, being silent. She didn't talk much at all. She used to hum and moan sometimes, particularly in the room by herself. She would do this little "ummhmm" like she was answering a question that nobody had even asked. Sometimes I would walk past the room and hear my grandma in there agreeing with herself or agreeing with God about something, but with just that "ummhmm," and that's all. As a young girl, I didn't understand why my grandmother didn't speak. And when she did talk, it was very brief—just to answer a question or ask if you needed something. Her mumbling words would pass through her gritted teeth in a small, southern drawl. She was very quiet, very specific, and very direct.

My grandmother Bernice, in her silence, taught me so much about self-care and about my own personal wellness. When I was growing up, I watched her be so still, so silent, so quiet, so sovereign, and so focused on whatever her day was about. That lady used to go to bed as soon as it started getting dark outside. I'm not talking about eight thirty or nine thirty p.m. I'm talking about six o'clock. It was starting to get dark outside, and Bernice Gully Moore was going to get in that bed, and/or she was going to disappear from the front of the house to the back of the house. She was done for the day. She also used to sit and rock her body and moan and hum. She loved sitting on the front porch in the sun. The language of sovereignty, honestly, feels so appropriate in the context of my grandmother Bernice because she just was her own. She was the exact opposite of my maternal grandmother, Emma Jane Baxley.

Emma Jane used to talk, laugh hard and long, was vibrant, full of energy, sometimes petty, sometimes shady, and hilarious. She participated in our shenanigans, and she didn't. She was about that life, and she absolutely wasn't. And then, well into her eighties, she all of a sudden just stopped talking. On the days when she would say anything, it was a big deal. Like, call the whole family, send a group text, family prayer praise report, big deal. That's how infrequently she spoke until she transitioned into the eternal.

I remember her starting to walk bent over like the weight of the world was on her shoulders, and then she was not walking as much anymore. And then she was confined to that bed. And then that was it. She never got back out of that bed. I don't remember my grandmother's words easing out. It felt like one day she was singing. One day she was humming. One day she was making a swift "uh un" sound to the great-grandkids as her way of saying sit down somewhere without words. And then nothing.

I never really thought about it, but maybe that's the reason why it was so hard to experience her verbal decline. I grew up with one grandmother who never spoke and a grandmother who talked all the time and then stopped. That silence felt like a reminder that I would never hear either of the voices of my grandmothers ever again.

Grandmother Emma Jane would wake up praying and praising. On her way to the bathroom, she'd jokingly sing through the living room, trying to distract us from seeing her wrapped in a towel. Except, she only brought more attention to herself by the way she hopped her grandmother-self through the house singing this little "boop boop boop boop boop boop boop." Shortly after, she would come out of her bedroom fully dressed, singing a song of praise and worship through the house before getting something to drink (always water or decaffeinated coffee). After enjoying her morning beverage, she would sit down in her chair that was perfectly positioned to be able to see out the front door and the side window, which is where she would rest for long stretches of time just sitting there quietly observing both the goings-on of the neighborhood and nature.

When I think about the lessons on sovereignty, wholeness, and being in my body that my grandmothers taught me, there is very early messaging around self-care long before the time we knew anything about the language of mindfulness. The ability to sit and watch a sunset on my own—I got that from Bernice. The intentionality of waking up early so that some part of the day belongs to me alone—I got that from Emma Jane Baxley. The rock of the body, the sway—I got that from Bernice. The humming and the singing—I got that from them both.

And while neither of them ever, that I know of, took a yoga class or went to an ashram and practiced meditation, their lives were a deep meditation and intentional mindfulness practice that sustained them during years that were very obviously troubling and hard and wracked with pain and sickness and disease.

Both of my grandmothers' silences remind me of part 2.2 in the definition of womanism as put forth by Alice Walker in her book *In Search of Our Mothers' Gardens*: "not a separatist, except periodically, for times of health." I may never be able to answer the question of whether silence was their self-care because I never asked Bernice, "Why do you say so few words?" and I never asked Emma Jane Baxley, "Why aren't you talking?" But I do know that my own relationship with silence was formed in the observation of their silence, and it has always served me in verbose ways. From watching them have a life-time's worth of practice that seemed to center some private time for themselves, it feels like it would be irresponsible to suggest that some of that silence wasn't intentional. Of course, not all of it because my grandmother Bernice suffered a stroke at some point when my dad was still a teenager. And my grandmother Emma Jane Baxley was diagnosed with dementia in her early eighties, so my understanding is that both of those illnesses and diagnoses impacted their health in such a way that their ability to speak was impacted as well.

But also, when you live a lifetime full of self-care practices and rituals, there is something about "deciding" not to say words for long stretches of time in your life—and that being both consequential and intentional. "Not a separatist, except periodically, for times of health" is an affirmation and confirmation that Black women need space to be silent and by themselves, both individually and as a collective for the sake of emotional and mental refreshment as well as for the body.

Prior to the silence that came after her stroke, my grandmother Bernice had endured emotional and physical abuse and then spent a good portion of her life after that not saying many words. Prior to my grandmother Emma Jane Baxley's years of silence, she had spent her life carrying the earth on her shoulders by raising her six daughters, helping to raise their children, and then being called the mother or the grandmother of pretty much every single person I've ever met in her time of living. Whether intentional or not, the silence of holding something, specifically her voice in this case, to herself to have something for herself can't be thrown away as coincidental, accidental, or just a result of her health. I saw both of my grandmothers use silence as an internal self-care practice that was neither purchased, earned, or rationed, and they used silence in both sickness and health.

I have been thinking about the Proverbs 31 woman: "She rises early." The scripture about this virtuous woman is one we're taught as young women in the church. She becomes this archetype. The way that we talk about her is usually in reference to her children and her husband. They call her good, but nobody ever makes the consideration that she rises early because she needs a minute to herself. What made me come to this womanist interpretation and understanding of that text was thinking about my grandmother Emma Jane Baxley, who never lived in or even slept in the house by herself from the time of her oldest child being born until the last day that she took a breath on this earth. Somebody was always spending the night at that house. Usually there were several grandchildren spending the night at any given time, which meant that my grandmother had very little time or space for herself. It could be easy for me to just be like, *Yes, my grandmother traditionally and historically had a practice of waking up early, always. That was a part of her practice.* But what I know for sure is that my grandmother woke up before all of the rest of us woke up, before she needed to go and make breakfast for the rest of us, and before she needed to get things together for whatever was happening in the day for us. She had that time for herself on purpose.

My grandmother Bernice was a ninja with how she took care of us and her home. You could be in the shower and get out to find that your dirty clothes, which you took off to get into the shower and left on the floor, had disappeared and were already in the washing machine or on their way to the clothesline before the water had evaporated from your freshly showered body. She was always so busy, and then she would keep that consistent ritual of rising early and disappearing when the sun was about to go down. She seemed to do that to have some time for herself.

It feels important to acknowledge all of the nuances that life forced both of them into—silence and stillness. It also feels essential to acknowledge what intentional pieces of silence they snatched for themselves solely because they needed something for themselves, being women who were expected to support the development and growth in the upbringing of their children, their grandchildren, the neighborhood, the community, and the folk.

Being in pursuit of wellness (and in the presence of wellness) for Black women is revolutionary. It is profound and transformative when Black women grab hold of pieces of something for themselves, and it's just for them. What is the one thing that can be solely for you, but you? Everything else somebody can come and try to snatch from you. "I bought this house for myself." Somebody's going to come try to spend the night. "I bought these chairs for myself." Somebody's gonna come try to sit in them. "I bought these lamps for myself." Somebody else is going to experience the brightening of the room as a result of them. But my time for myself where I take care of myself, which is not a thing that has been taught or preached or practiced in any way, shape, form, or fashion to me, is absolutely resistance. I resist and reject and refuse the idea that I, as a Proverbs 31 woman, am "good" *for* my husband and my children's benefit and not that I am "good" for myself. I refuse that. I am "good" because I am good to myself first.

Audre Lorde said, "Caring for myself is not self-indulgence. It is self-preservation. And that is an act of political warfare." A possible fourth-wave womanist would ask the question, "What if the by-product of the work of the Proverbs 31 woman is that she is 'good' to everyone else and everything else because she has a deep practice of self-indulgence and self-preservation? What if she ain't thinking about that man or those kids when she gets up early, but because she has centered herself, everybody else just so happens to benefit?" Decentering them and centering her IS the womanist work happening here. She rises early for herself. And as a result of her being full, they get to enjoy the spoils of a whole and well woman. Of course, freedom is the point, but freedom and wellness aren't mutually exclusive. You actually can't have one without the other.

The goal is not for you to take care of yourself so that you can march and sign more petitions and do other work, because the goal of getting well isn't to have more endurance for marches and protests. We got to do that anyway because real liberation demands action and praxis: abolition, policy change, leadership shifting, and dismantling. But my grandmothers practiced wellness while serving as matriarchs who experienced all kinds of traumas. Without their wellness, there would be no EbonyJanice! Our sheer existence and ability to explore our pleasures is evidence that the wellness of our elders is the well from which our liberation hydrates. So here we are, a wave of Black womanist thinkers and scholars who are asserting, "If we never sign another petition, we are not less worthy of the freedom we find at the end of this journey than anyone else, since getting to the finish line was the whole point all along."

In *The Color Purple*, Miss Sophia walks up to Celie and asks the question, "You told Harpo to beat me?" (Alice Walker). It becomes clear at some point that to downplay the violence that is happening to her, and likely as a way to cope with it, Celie says to Miss Sofia, "Trouble don't last always. Heaven be here soon." To which Miss Sophia replies, "You ought to knock Mister over the head and worry about Heaven later." *Wellness is the work* is the fourth-wave womanist's way of saying, *We're going to worry about Heaven later because we are going to be free NOW.* We cannot wait for Heaven to know what it feels like to experience liberation in this body.

Audre Lorde further offered that "the body is political for Black people," so self-care is the act of ensuring we get to be free. There is no relationship to Black bodies on this continent separate from politicization. The body of the Black person is here in the United States of America as a result of something political. It was made legal to bring this body here. It was made legal to force this body to do what it was forced to do. It was made legal to kill the Black body. It was made legal to exploit the Black body. So caring for this Black body is a way to subvert the politics that has historically exploited this political site that is constantly in resistance just by existing.

The pursuit of wellness as it pertains to Black women is a radical act of resistance because, historically, this body, a political site, has not ever legally been able to rest, experience ease, or pursue pleasure as its primary focus and purpose. To pursue rest, ease, wellness, and pleasure as my primary focus in this political body is a justice reclamation, and that contributes to this movement.

We don't actually talk enough as a community about how much resistance we really have to the idea of self-care being a necessary part of an integral contribution to Black liberation. I have seen so much critique of, including language around, self-care as an integral (not as a supplemental) contribution to the freedom movement we are all in just as a result of being in these bodies and wanting to be able to survive. And some of the critique is that you cannot *day spa* yourself into freedom. That you cannot *luxury vacation* yourself into freedom. That you cannot *mani and pedi* yourself into freedom. And I want to be crystal clear that I don't disagree with that. I do not believe that going to a day spa is going to get you free, but what I do need to say is that to minimize the impact of the day spa, the mani pedi, the decision to sit down somewhere and just take care of yourself, to be lavish, to be luxurious, and to pamper yourself as if it is not a radical act is ill-informed. We live in a world, particularly as it pertains to Black women, that does not have any space for us to be well. It does not have any space for us to relax. There is no space for Black women to be chilling. So the decision to invest in your rest, relaxation, and total wellness can be part of that radical and revolutionary journey.

Historically, this Black feminine form has been expected to be beaten, scorned, abused, sexualized, have no autonomy, not be considered feminine, and not be considered worthy of protection, care, gentleness, or softness. So when a Black woman, in this form, makes the intentional decision to be like, "Oh, no, no, no, by any means necessary, I'm going to be lavish with myself," that is in stark contrast to what the political site of this body has historically had access to. Is it the only way? No. You are not going to solely *day spa* yourself into liberation. That would require privilege that we all do not have access to. But to assert that it is not a part of this sacred journey at all and that there's nothing revolutionary about making that choice? No, that's not real either.

I found a picture of my grandmother Emma Jane Baxley napping a couple years ago. I do not know for sure if she's napping, but it looks like she's lying on the couch, which is such a big deal to me and my cousins because my grandmother used to be like, "Quit wallowing on my couch." You had to sit up straight and be still on that couch. She's from Alabama; we don't actually know if she was saying "wallowing" or "waddling" or some other word. But don't do it. Whatever it is. Don't do that on her couch. Period. So to see this picture of my grandmother lying across this couch with one of her arms thrown back and the hem of her night shirt slightly lifted to show her soft belly was mind blowing. She may be napping; she may just be lying there being silly because that is who Emma Jane Baxley was, but I never saw her do that in my life until I found that photo. Now I frequent womanist conversations with my mother and my aunt Phyllis about who I would be if I ever saw my grandmother napping. Who would I be if I ever saw any of her six daughters being lavish with the care for themselves? If my mother had a wellness practice that was the central theme of her life? Or my elders had a nap regiment, a day spa savings, a self-care routine that included being luxurious and sometimes frivolous with themselves? If they didn't have to be so responsible, so put together, so grown and womanish? Who would we be if we had seen that with our eyes when we were growing up? It is transformative just to consider this. Just to imagine this.

To see my elders, whose bodies are also political sites that have historically been seen as for labor and reproduction, doing nothing is to see something that I have never seen. That is revolutionary. But I am not just talking about going to the spa, wearing a face mask, taking a long bath, getting your manicure and pedicure, even though you're absolutely worthy of and deserving of all of those things, especially because, historically, Black women have not had the kinds of privileges or access that would make it possible to center those types of rituals of self-care.

When I speak of wellness, I am thinking of the intentional, revolutionary work of Tricia Hersey of The Nap Ministry, who is building on the work of our elders such as Audre Lorde and June Jordan. June Jordan saw self-care as self-preservation. In her 1978 address to the Black Writers Conference at Howard University, she said, "I am a feminist, and what that means to me is much the same as the meaning of the fact that I am Black. It means that I must undertake to love myself and to respect myself as though my very life depends on self-love and self-respect. It means that I must everlastingly seek to cleanse myself of hatred and the contempt that surrounds and permeates my identity as a woman and as a Black human being in this

particular world of ours." This act of self-love and self-respect is integral to the work of The Nap Ministry. There is powerful theory, ethic,
and practice that Tricia Hersey is implementing as she continues to
add and contribute to this important ideology. That rest is the "work"
and is the main theme that she continues to affirm on an ongoing basis
when teaching this practice.

When I say that wellness is the central essential tool of liberation,
I'm also speaking of Lauren Ash and the work of Black Girl in Om,
which centers Black women's wellness as the tool to get us closer to
freedom by asking the question, "What tools do Black women need to
just be able to breathe easy?" That is the work. If Black women have
traditionally and historically not been able to do something, and then
somebody contributes to work that supports them in being able to do
something, that is revolution; that is revolutionary. That is a tool for
freedom.

I'm further thinking about the work of Shelah Marie from Curvy,
Curly, Conscious, who was one of the first people I ever heard talk
about the importance of Black women being able to just play. That may
seem frivolous when you think about the work of the elders and the
ancestors who were marching in protest and having dogs sicked on
them or having fire hydrants turned on them, but it also is the reason
why you were seeing pictures of a forty-two-year-old Rosa Parks looking like a grandmother. That's the reason why Martin Luther King Jr.
historically looked like he was in his fifties. This man was thirty-nine
years old when he was assassinated.

If I had seen pictures of Mary McLeod Bethune taking a nap or
Dorothy Height doing yoga or Angela Davis Hula-Hooping . . . If I
had experienced my grandmother and my aunts skating and jumping
rope and playing freeze tag and playing in makeup and having access
to that type of joviality on an ongoing basis, not just in the pockets of
life but in the overflow of living . . . If I saw elder Black women get to

be light and soft and not have to be serious all the time to be taken seriously, who and where would I be?

I'm talking about pleasure and bliss in the work of Thea Monyeé, who is asking the questions about pleasure and bliss in every single area of our lives. When pleasure has been historically stripped from your reality, there is no preachment or teaching or passing along of language around pleasure or bliss as a central theme. Therefore, to center it is revolutionary.

When I say wellness is the work, I'm thinking of Roya Marsh, who is a pioneer in furthering the discussion of Black joy as resistance. We know that Black joy is so important because summer 2020 showed us that Black pain is the catalyst upon which most allies show up. But if my pain is the only thing that gets you to move, then I'll always have to be dying for change to happen. Therefore, to center Black joy is revolutionary because my joy has to become the trigger that makes allies get up out of their seats and run towards freedom. Black joy is so important because, again, we cannot wait to get to Heaven to know what it feels like to experience joy. We need and deserve that now. And that wellness is a central tool and is the work that sustains us in this pursuit.

This also makes me think of Jade T. Perry and her work that demands we think about Black people with disabilities and chronic illnesses and the relationship that we all share, regardless of our ability. She constantly reminds us that Black disabled folk must be one of the mirrors through which we gauge how near or far we actually are from freedom. This teaches me that I cannot separate my freedom from other Black folks with various other marginalized identities because the only way all Black people are truly free is if all Black people are truly free.

I mean it when I say that this is the work and these are the tools. Being in pursuit of wellness is one way of saying that when

Black women shift towards wholeness, wellness, self-care, and self-preservation as the primary way of being, that is revolutionary because, historically, we have not been able to do that, so much so that we even have tension with this conversation amongst ourselves.

I grew up in church singing, "*We are soldiers in the army. We have to fight although we have to cry. We have to hold up the bloodstained banner. We have to hold it up until we die.*" We've got to hold it up until we die? We don't never get a break from holding it up? "*My mother, she was a soldier. Oh, yes. She put her hand on a gospel plow. Oh, yes. But one day she got old. She couldn't fight anymore. She said, 'I stand here and fight anyhow.' Oh, we are soldiers in the army.*" Can I get old and not have to stand here and fight anyhow? Is there never any rest or reprieve? So in the context of our own socialization, even inside of Black girlhood and Black womanhood, there is no space for rest; there is no space for playing.

Black girls be so serious. Black girls be so grown, and that's what the world expects from Black girls—to be responsible, to be strong, to be serious, to be reserved, to know how to act, to stand here and fight anyhow, even though I'm tired. Now of course we know historically, our elders had to stand there and fight anyhow because death was imminent, but this pursuit of wellness as the tool is also to heal our ancestors. Angela Davis said, "For a long time, activists did not necessarily think that it mattered to take care of themselves in terms of what they eat, in terms of mental self-care, corporal self-care, spiritual self-care. I know that there were some people who emphasized it. I'm thinking about one of the leaders of the Black Panther Party, Ericka Huggins, who began to practice yoga and meditation in the seventies. And she encouraged many people including Huey Newton and Bobby Seale to join that practice. I think they did a little bit of it, but I think that movement would have been very different had we understood the importance of that kind of self-care." This proves that we're building on the work of the elders around incorporating self-care into our justice work, but essentially, Angela Davis herself even affirms what the movement would have or could have been if self-care was centered. If we had a whole bunch of healthier, more clear, emotionally mature leaders, how much more sustainable would that work have been? It was not supplemental.

In order to embrace what the elders have sprinkled into their work, we have to decolonize our minds and internal socialized belief systems around what we deserve and are worthy of.

My grandmothers didn't have the language of self-care or wellness. They were just trying to keep a "reasonable portion" of their "right mind." They consciously chose the path that led to rest, and there is much to learn there. I want to choose my silence. I do not want it forced upon me because the world decided that Black girl magic was for everyone except for the Black girl performing the miracles. May my best miracles be tucked away for me in my early morning rising, which is absolutely for my own revolutionary self. We deserve that. We are worthy of that as well.

IN PURSUIT OF
MY NAME

"My name is EbonyJanice. I go by EbonyJanice.
Which means you should call me EbonyJanice."
—EBONYJANICE

I have historically gone by EbonyJanice. It is the actual name that my mother gave me, and I have been introducing myself as EbonyJanice since primary school. I have always loved and had an intimate relationship with my whole name. As I've gotten older, the profundity of being named after both my maternal grandmother, Emma Jane Baxley, and my paternal grandmother, Bernice Moore, is even more distinct to me. There are levels and layers to my name. EJ is from Emma Jane, and Janice, which looks like *Jan-nis* but is absolutely pronounced like *Juh-nees*, is from my grandmother Bernice. I've loved to share my own definition of my name since I was a little girl—Ebony (Black) Janice (Gift from God)—obsessed with the fact that when my aunt Pat suggested "Ebony" to my mother as a name for me, it was specifically because of her love for Blackness. Why would I ever shorten my name? Why would I ever lean into a public nickname with a name like EbonyJanice?

While some people who know me very well have been able to get away with calling me Ebony, a good majority of my childhood friends have always called me EbonyJanice and still do to this day. Especially because, even as a child, I would correct you if you didn't say my whole name, and because Janice looks like it should be pronounced *Jan-nis*, I would stop and be like, "It's Janice [*Juh-nees*]." I've never let a moment slide by that I didn't make that correction or that distinction. Ever.

As I started to do more public scholarship work, I introduced myself as EbonyJanice and let others know they should call me EbonyJanice. It also felt important to me because there are so many Ebonys in the world. To ensure that we know whom we're talking about, I go by EbonyJanice. I even go by Ebony no-space Janice, EbonyJanice. One name. Then, at some point (you can see this on past books that I have self-published), I started going by ebonyjanice—all lowercase and one word—because I also felt the capital letters were making it look like those were two different names when the reality is, I wanted it to be very clear that it was all one name—EbonyJanice. When my work was starting to become more public, people would show up in my comment section calling me Ebony. I took the opportunity to correct them to the point that when I started doing live workshops, live events, live lectures, and social media lives, I started by saying, "My name is EbonyJanice. I go by EbonyJanice." A couple of seconds later, somebody would be in the comment section or coming up to me afterwards saying, "Ebony, that was amazing." It was like, whatever I said at the beginning was wiped away. So I escalated my introduction across all platforms to, "My name is EbonyJanice. I go by EbonyJanice, which means that you should call me EbonyJanice."

And still, people try to call me Ebony.

Would a student walk into the back of a Harvard classroom and scream, "Hi, Joe!" to the professor? Not unless he specifically asked the students to call him that. And even then, the student would address the professor by the name the professor wished to be called. The assertion, or the idea, that it is ever acceptable, under any circumstances, to change someone's name without permission or an intimate, communal relationship is outright disrespect.

And to be clear, more often than not, it's white people calling me Ebony. The historical implications of white people renaming others has a deep-rooted relationship with their colonizing ancestors' behaviors. I don't have to provide corrections more than once for most people of color. But for non-POCs, there is a great tension with the idea that "I introduced myself as EbonyJanice. Call me EbonyJanice." But the great privilege of whiteness is that folk grow up in an arrogance that suggests they can say whatever name they want to.

Even if my name seems too complicated, the inability to conceive a person having two names is lazy, at best. White people commonly have *two* names: John Michael, Mary Kate, Billy Bob. I've never heard Mary-Kate Olsen called anything but Mary-Kate Olsen—ever—and there's no tension with it. But let me pull up on the scene, consistently for years saying, "My name is EbonyJanice. I go by EbonyJanice," and suddenly tongues get heavy and lips get to fumbling over those teeth.

I know too many Black women scholars in academia who have students who will full-blown attempt to call them by their first names. Meanwhile, they go by Doctor or Professor or have asked to be called XYZ, but students have insisted on calling them whatever it is they want to call them, and more often than not, they do not do that same thing to male faculty—most specifically white faculty, and especially white male faculty.

I've experienced it firsthand. I have heard my white colleagues called by whatever name with a handle on the front. And then I have been relegated to not even my whole first name by students. That's going to be a problem every single time. I'm going to call it out. I'm going to name it. To not call me EbonyJanice is an erasure of my mother's impactful intention when she gifted me my name. I'm going to take the moment, and we will sit in discomfort together because I'm never, in this lifetime or the next, going to be uncomfortable about students or people on social media calling me something other than what I have asked to be called.

That refusal is radical resistance. That is freedom-making. That is movement.

For various reasons, people of color just tend to understand that. We share a history of our culture stripped from us through misnaming or renaming or being forced into assimilation. Because there is a likelihood that someone has misnamed us at some point or another, it's less of a trigger to be corrected about somebody's name. And Black people have an intimate familiarity with having to whitewash or water down our existence in one form or another.

Things fare no better for immigrants in the United States of America who have names indigenous to their native lands. Uzoamaka Nwanneka Aduba, known for her role as Crazy Eyes in *Orange Is the New Black*, told an audience of teenage girls at a *Glamour* magazine event a fitting story. She recalled the time she was trying to convince her Nigerian mom that, rather than belabor her classmates and others with learning and pronouncing her full name, it would be better for her parents to call her Zoe so others would call her that as well. Her mother responded, "If they can learn to say Tchaikovsky and Michelangelo and Dostoevsky, then they can learn to say Uzoamaka." Aduba reflected on the impact of this moment with her mother by telling her audience, "And what is amazing now standing in my womanhood and in my power is, I wouldn't change my name for a second. I am so proud of that name and what stands behind it and what it represents. So do not ever erase those identifiers that are held in you . . . whether it's your name . . . it is yours. It was given to you at birth, and it is yours to own."

The world will use what we call ourselves against us as often as possible. So when you apply for a job with the name Bettyna, Krishonda, Felicia, or Shaquana, there is an automatic assumption that you are Black, and therefore, your name can be used against you. Of those names I just mentioned, which are real people I know, I want to say that three out of four of them use an alternate version of their name when they apply for jobs—an initial and then their middle name. So, instead of Krishonda, K. Nicole. Instead of Shaquana, Shawn. Instead of Felicia, middle name Marie. The need to do that is a violence that gets grazed over because we assume that the other aggressions we experience are of a higher importance. What can be more violent than not being able to be called the name that your family assigned to you and that your community calls you daily?

There is a deeply historical relationship associated with needing very basic things, like employment and acceptance into certain spaces, and forcing the renaming of Black people so they can have access to those basic things, which creates a reality where basic naming is a justice issue. We were brought to this continent as a result of chattel slavery. A part of colonization is to change the name of a thing. We see the changing of names with people and land. This happens with gentrification. Even at this present moment, a segment of Harlem is being called NoHo, a very intentional violence to uproot and disrupt that space. We can look to the famous and grotesque scene in Alex Haley's *Roots*, where Kunta Kinte is being beaten for refusing to adopt the name the white man gave him. As the slaver is attempting to whip Kunta Kinte into submission, he is demanding Kinte repeat his slave name, which is Toby. And he just gets beat because he refuses to say "Toby" and is holding on for dear life to "My name is Kunta Kinte" because of the relationship with his native land and people who gave him that name and because of the story attached to that name when it was assigned to him.

There is an ongoing expectation that Black people, in general, will accept whatever name has been ascribed to them because that is how colonization works. There is an imperialistic mentality that, across land and sea, whatever white supremacist delusion names or ascribes to a thing is what it is. The refusal to call himself Toby, even though that could have meant his very life, is what made that moment in *Roots* so profound. The people standing around who loved him, cared about him, or just didn't want to see this violent thing happening even contributed to this socialization. "Just say Toby. Just say Toby." They believed that if Kunta just said "Toby," it would keep him from being harmed; it would keep him safe. Many people who allow for a variation of their names believe that it will keep them from experiencing a certain kind of violence on another day. They believe that just saying "Toby" will change the oppressors' perspective of them as resistant, as belligerent, and as someone who will cause trouble if they just make it easy for them. *Just say Toby.*

Some parents go so far as to give their children "white-adjacent" names in an attempt to avoid harm. This is a form of respectability politics. Because in that moment of watching Kunta Kinte get beaten for saying his name, you are socialized into believing, *I don't want to create an environment or reality or life for my children where they will be harmed or miss out on opportunities or just not be safe or accepted because their name is not acceptable in this context.* But there is little evidence to prove that just saying "Toby" increases the likelihood of ongoing safety. In fact, everyone standing around begging Kunta to "Just say Toby" had experienced their own fates of violence. The very nature of having to watch Kunta be beat for wanting to hold on to his name was violence in itself.

Alice Walker coined the language of "womanist." Walker had used the term "womanist" in her review of *Gifts of Power: The Writings of Rebecca Jackson, Black Visionary, Shaker Eldress* with an edited introduction by Jean McMahon Humez. Rebecca Jackson had a unique conversion experience and left her husband, vowing celibacy and living her life in close relationship with another Black femme in a religious community known as Shakers. The editor, Jean McMahon Humez, names this relationship that Rebecca and the Shaker sister had as a lesbian relationship. Alice Walker's position on this assumption was that Humez made some gross assertions in this framing by disregarding Jackson's vow of celibacy and interpreting her relationship with her Shaker sister as anything more than sisterhood. Further, Walker insisted that labeling Rebecca Jackson as lesbian took away part of Jackson's agency because, as Black women, naming ourselves is the "least we can do." Walker believed that being able to name ourselves may be the only tangible sign of personal freedom for Black women in this society. Alice Walker was saying, first of all, no one has the authority to call these women lesbians based on what one decides is truth. Unless you are a Black woman, you are an observer of Black women's relationships. Rebecca Jackson and the Shaker sister never name themselves lesbians. Walker says, "At the very least, we should be able to name ourselves."

From Walker's profound statement comes the four-part definition of womanism that we have been considering throughout the entirety of this text. A part of that naming created space for thinking through what it would mean to call ourselves womanist—a very specific, Black, sociopolitical, and spiritual-religious framework that gave tools and theory around Black women's existence—and hopes to answer some of the questions of the who, what, when, where, why, and how of Black womanhood. A major part of that work, which Walker is considering a liberative tool, is naming.

In author Yaa Gyasi's debut book, entitled *Homegoing*, the reader meets a character named H, a Ghanaian descendant of a family that has been enslaved in the USA. He gets into an argument with his girlfriend, Ethe. He calls Ethe by a different woman's name, and then she breaks up with him. Soon thereafter, H is falsely arrested for "studyin' a white woman," or simply for allegedly speaking to a white woman. He is imprisoned for ten years because he couldn't pay a ten-dollar fine. Upon his release, he reaches back out to Ethe and explains that the main reason he didn't call her was because he was embarrassed about the way they broke up. Ethe explains what hurt her the most about their breakup:

You have to understand, H, the day you called me that woman's name I thought, Ain't I been through enough? Ain't just about everything I ever had been taken away from me? My freedom. My family. My body. And now I can't even own my name. Ain't I deserve to be Ethe to you, at least, if nobody else?

She continues:

My mama gave me that name herself. All I had of her, then, was my name. That was all I had of myself, too. And you wouldn't even give me that.

I sobbed when I read this passage. Here I am, roughly 140 years after the Reconstruction Era, which is the timeline of this passage, and I am still fighting for my freedom, my family, my body, and my name.

Ain't I deserve to be EbonyJanice at the very least?

The power of a name is an affirmation of one's worthiness. To pronounce a name incorrectly is giving *lazy*, and it's serving, *I'ma call you what I want to call you, and I don't care if this is embarrassing.* Calling somebody by their name is doing the basic work of being able to empathize with what it is like for someone who has historically been stereotyped or dismissed because of their name. It is powerful work to insist that you say my name correctly. It is equally revolutionary for you to be intentional and careful with people about their name. When I taught undergrad, I took a moment to figure out students' names. Tahzhane'y. "Tah-juh-nay," I said. This class was on Zoom, and I watched her sit up in her bed and say, "This is the first time in my entire school experience that a teacher has gotten my name right on the first day of class." She looked a little weepy for a moment as if to say, *How am I in my twenties, and this is the first time somebody in academia has pronounced my name right?*

When the class was complete and I was done working for that university, Tahzhane'y went on to become an intern for The Free People Project. I sincerely believe that relationship was made possible by me taking a breath before attempting her name on the first day of class.

Naming and nicknaming is important to this conversation because people go by various names, but there's something about being invited into that very intimate and specific reality. I actually have several nicknames, but there are individuals who are the only individuals on the planet who can call me that specific name because that is the relationship agreement.

For example, I have a cousin who grew up being called Doonk Doonk, and when we were children, that was the agreement—that he could be called Doonk Doonk. And then he got to the place where he desired to be called by his actual name—the name that his mother and father gave him—and that agreement from our childhood changed. He had more clarity about how he wanted to be known, and it became our responsibility to see his sovereignty enough to call him what he asked to be called, even if we were used to calling him something else.

In one of my favorite Toni Morrison books, *Song of Solomon*, there is a character who was referred to as "Milkman" because somebody saw him getting breastfed at an age that was determined as way too old. Even though he went along with it, there was always a humiliation attached to the name Milkman. A nickname indicates familiarity and usually comes with the historical relationship to the story of that name. Therefore, anybody who is outside of that agreement, or that intimate structure, has no right to assume that they can call him that unless he's introduced himself to them as Milkman. This means, even if you hear other people calling someone by a certain name, unless they have invited you into that reality, it could be emotionally violent for you to misname them.

My father calls me "Dawter," "Miss Mo," or "Mama." Wouldn't it be odd for a stranger to duplicate my dad's nicknames for me? There is an intimate knowing and agreement about those nicknames that have context that others cannot know if they have not been invited into that knowing. Most people in marginalized identities tend to understand that calling someone by a name other than the name that they've introduced themselves as requires consent. Holding our names as sacred is a revolutionary act of resistance and worthy of consideration from the inside and out.

* * *

As I mentioned previously, I worked at the front desk of the seminary school I attended in Berkeley, California. One afternoon, a white female classmate, who absolutely knew my name, came in the front door and didn't acknowledge me until she needed something from me. She came back to the front desk and said, "Ebony, something, something, something, something, something." I replied, "My name is EbonyJanice." We had a stare-off. Without saying my name, she restated her request. She said, "Can you help me with something, something, something?" I repeated, "My name is EbonyJanice." I sat there waiting for her to make a choice. She shifted from one foot to the other and let out a little huff. As she was reaching to pull her white-woman tears and belligerence off the shelf, another classmate, who happened to be lying under my desk playing with my dog, stood up, appearing out of nowhere, and asked, "Why do you have an attitude when you won't just say this woman's name?" The one who had refused to say my name looked shocked; her face shone bright red through her defeated embarrassment, and as she held back tears, she finally said, "*EbonyJanice.*"

I implore you—just stare. Correct them. And wait. This is resistance. I'm not finna use my best magic every day for the basic expectation of being called my name. I'm not going to have to plead the blood of Jesus and call on the Holy Ghost and conjure just for my name. I'm not marching to Selma or getting a petition signed just to be called what my mother named me. When others assume this action is angry, unnecessary, or petty, stand on the wise words of Linnethia "NeNe" Leakes: "I said what I said."

IN PURSUIT OF
MADNESS

"If you are silent about your pain,
they'll kill you and say you enjoyed it."
—ZORA NEALE HURSTON

I feel physically ill when I think back over my life and consider all the times something hurt me, offended me, and caused harm to me, but for the sake of not ruffling any feathers, I did not make any noise. I didn't say "ouch" when it hurt. I didn't flinch. I didn't let out a heavy sigh. I held my face in an impassive expression, and I was "strong." I didn't let them get to me. I didn't let them sway me. I didn't say anything.

At the time, it was always because I knew, even as a young girl, that Black girl madness was not allowed. Black girls can't scream, can't cuss, can't fuss, can't sob, can't kick, can't punch, can't wallow, can't be in a rage. Why? Because either nobody believes in our pain because "Black girls are strong" or because "mad Black girls are dangerous," and nobody is safe around a dangerous Black girl.

The more I pursue true liberation, the more I think of Zora Neale Hurston's quote, "If you are silent about your pain, they'll kill you and say you enjoyed it." It makes me wonder—how much was my controlled response leading people to believe that I was not in pain? Also, where did all the rage go that I did not give to the moment?

In her album *A Seat at the Table*, Solange sang my lived experience. From track to track, it was the most cohesive explanation of my Black girl life that I had ever heard on record to that point. Three years later, her next album, *When I Get Home*, came out. In the first song on the album, she repeats for a minute and fifty-nine seconds: "I saw things I imagined." I immediately wondered, *How did Solange go from* A Seat at the Table *in which she is expressing being weary of the ways of the world to seeing things she imagined on* When I Get Home? It was while I was relistening to the song "Mad" on *A Seat at the Table* that something clicked for me. The words "I got a lot to be mad about" made me consider how the decision to be mad is a radical act. It is revolutionary for Black girls to access and explore their madness.

Let's be clear. When I use the word "mad," I am not speaking of petty bitterness; I am referring to my righteous anger. More specifically, I am speaking to my right to be furious, incensed, and exhausted by the unlivable conditions this world offers my blackity Black girl self on the daily. I am talking about being in pursuit of the space to express myself when I am vexed and to do so without suffering social sanction.

There is a trope we avoid like the plague: "Angry Black Woman." One way that Black women avoid the stereotype of being viewed as angry is to code-switch. Code-switching is a set of behaviors that includes changing the pitch and tone of our voice to sound "friendlier." By definition, code-switching is a change in language, behavior, or appearance, and it is a social behavior used to show assimilation with dominant societal norms and values. We often code-switch so that we don't fall into the violent, racist, misogynistic trope of being "Angry Black Women" (as if Black women have no rights to their anger).

Pursuing madness demonstrates that I've never had a right to access madness. What space is there for a Black girl to be mad? Society and even our families will use our anger against us. The perpetuation of the Angry Black Woman trope doesn't come exclusively at the hands of nonblack people, however. The violent narrative is so deeply ingrained in society that even some Black men believe that Black women are inherently bitter. So many of us code-switch out of our anger, our madness, our frustration, and our bitterness on a regular basis because we have been socialized into the idea that "mad" is who we are and all we'll ever be. We have grown to associate our "madness" with the pain of loss and isolation that comes as a result of accessing those feelings. So Black women reject the feeling altogether to avoid being pigeonholed into a stereotypical Black girl. At the same time, some of us fall so hard into madness that we don't have any space or room for anything else but rage.

Imagine living an existence where, as a means of protection and self-preservation, you avoid natural feelings of frustration and anger. Or conversely, imagine living an existence where people only expect madness from you and judge you for feeling this feeling that you have a natural right to feel. Solange's album *A Seat at the Table* can serve as guiding lyrics for Black women who need to find their angry voice and express displeasure. The album accompanies Black women who are "in pursuit of madness." To suppress our anger is actually violent to us and to our bodies. Solange says, "I got a lot to be mad about," and this is a powerful affirmation to all the Black girls and women listening to this album to acknowledge that we *do*, in fact, have a lot to be mad about. To consciously decide to be mad is transformative because avoiding a particular feeling for generations means that we have been missing out on whatever is produced when we properly process our emotions.

When I was in grad school, after I completed a semester-long presentation on "Black women's body ownership as a justice issue," one of my classmates, a white woman, tried to play the victim by calling out my body language while she was presenting. Number one, I wasn't thinking about that lady. Number two, I had *just* gotten done saying that my body is my own. She had no right to try to dictate what I did with my body. But she thought it was acceptable to insert her thoughts on how *my* body was making her feel.

When she acted like she was going to get up and leave the classroom because she didn't "feel held or safe in the space any longer," I stood up first and said, "Oh no you won't. I'm the one who was aggressed against. You harmed me. You don't get to storm out and be the victim—I do." And that's just what I did. I left and even slammed the door on my way out for emphasis. I had a right to that madness not just because of her behavior but also because the only person, in that moment, speaking up for this public violence that was happening to me was the only other Black person in the space. She deserved my madness, and they did too.

After several other violent aggressions towards my body at this institution, I publicly told them, "Do not say my name; I will not say your name." "You won't get any more photo ops with me." "Take my name off your website." "Take my face off your banners." "Do not use my image, my likeness, my name, my work, or anything that I contributed to this institution to promote this space in the future." My righteous anger pushed me to not only call them out but also to make sure the world knew, "I got a lot to be mad about at this institution."

A Black femme on the school's board of directors reached out to me to tell me, "Don't burn this bridge." This elder basically told me, "You know how these institutions are. You just gotta play the game." Let me tell you something. I ain't never burnt a bridge that I would want to walk back across. Ever. If anybody withdraws their support because

I'm telling the truth about not being safe there, then those are bridges that need to be burned to the ground. Elders in our community who want to suggest that our madness is not credible or valid when we express it ascribe to that ideology and behavior in an attempt to use our credible anger, disappointment, and frustration against us. I understand that may be the way they had to maneuver, and I hate that for them. I both empathize and feel deep gratitude for all the women and femmes that came before me who did their justice work in a nice suit, hat, and gloves. Thank you to the ones who said it gently and sweetly, who wore the appropriate undergarments, pantyhose, shapewear, and a slip, had their hair perfectly coiffed and pulled into a ponytail or bun or hanging down their shoulders bone straight. Thank you for everything you did to get me to this point where I can access my madness and burn those bridges to the ground. I wish you had the space to express your anger and quote Maurice Samuel "Trick Daddy" Young: "Bitch, I don't need you. No way. No how. Not then. Not now. Uh-uh."

The proof that I did the right thing by calling out my grad school for its failure to make me safe while still taking my hundreds of thousands of dollars is that, to this day, there has been no repair made from Starr King School for the Ministry. They have not repaired their harm to me, and they have not made a public repair of their harm to the other Black women who spoke out after I called them out for their harm to me. This says to me that I was right to burn that bridge because what would I look like walking back over to share my good name, my good gifts, and my great reputation with an institution that doesn't practice what that raggedy *Black Lives Matter* banner on the front of the building preaches? Gender-neutral girl, bye!

I continue to think deeply about my madness towards the status quo as my resistance to the fantastic hegemonic imaginative narrative. This resistance to the fantastic hegemonic imaginative narrative is a resistance to all institutions, not to the exclusion of the institution that is the church and even the institution that is my family. For example, there is a narrative about what it means to be a bald-headed or nappy-headed Black woman. When I first went natural, it went against the grain of my family, so I didn't get the support I would have liked. It was confusing to my family that I would actually want my hair to be nappy. It was confusing to my family when I cut my hair off into a fade for the first time. I had to tell people my hair is an off-limits conversation. I had to have an attitude at times. This was considered disrespectful to some of my elders, but without my madness, it would have remained easy to sweep the discussion of hair politics in our family under the rug and even easier to continue to disrespect my choice to look like I naturally do.

Eventually, nearly every person in my family would become natural as well. As a collective, we have divested from the madness that comes with our hair to the point that one of my preteen loved ones rocks a fade because she understands that "hair grows back" and has the model of "hair grows back" in her older cousin EbonyJanice, who has been bald-headed several times in her lifetime. While it wasn't easy when I first chose to be brave enough to get mad about my hair, in the end, it benefited not only me but my entire family. My madness has changed the trajectory of a beauty standard inside my family for generations to come.

Another example of how my *madness* is resistance is the way this madness is shifting the culture of homophobia inside my family. Years ago when North Carolina started ramping up its transphobic laws to police public restrooms, my father made some statements in agreement with the laws. As I attempted to educate him that his comments were inherently transphobic, he doubled down, and we ended up in a heated exchange that concluded with me telling him not to speak to me as long as he kept that kind of harmful truth in his heart. I went for days, in my father's house (where he paid the mortgage), not speaking to him. Even if he spoke to me, I did not speak back. Days passed before I finally approached my father and asked, "Are you done being an evil, transphobic, horrible person?" He shyly grinned and replied, "Yes, Daughter." To which I replied, "No you're not. But this is a start."

My madness and refusal to just "agree to disagree" with my father's transphobic beliefs started a dialogue in our family that would not have ever been possible if it weren't for the righteous rage of anger that changes things.

Lauryn Hill once said, "And even after all my logic and my theory, I add a 'motherfucker' so you ignorant niggas hear me." What we understand, when given permission to feel our frustration, our disappointment, and our rage, is that a lot of years of saying it cute, smart, and sweet only adds to the bitterness that sets in when we have no rights to our madness. The fact of the matter is, some folk do not hear you until you cuss . . . then things start moving and shaking. The pursuit of madness is both healing and transformative because I got a lot to be mad about, and I got a right to be mad about it.

IN PURSUIT OF
MY ANCESTORS

"Ancestors put me on game.
Ankh charm on gold chains, with my Oshun energy."
—BEYONCÉ

In December of 2015, I was doing a meditation at my altar in my bedroom, and my maternal grandmother, who was still alive at the time, visited me in the spirit and gave me a very clear message for my future. She said, "Stop being safe like I was. I wanted to be a writer. I stopped writing. Whatever you say you want to be, don't stop being that. Be who you say you are. Do what you say you're going to do. Don't be like us. Be brave." Two weeks later, my grandmother transitioned into the eternal and became my ancestor. Though I publicly wrote about this visitation before my grandmother left her flesh body, there is still tension for certain people in my family about me speaking of my grandmother as having visited me before she transitioned or speaking so publicly about her as an ancestor. In my Christian family, ancestral reverence is "demonic."

The reality, however, is that I had been hiding that I no longer identified as a Christian. My grandmother was the only elder in my family that knew I was in this peculiar spiritual space. In the midst of my theological shift, I happened to be in my hometown, Sandusky, Ohio, helping to care for her. Often, I would climb up next to her in her little hospice bed and talk her head off about the questions, concerns, and confusion I was having about the religion of my youth. Sometimes I would say really harsh things about Jesus while making the yikes emoji face, scared she was going to find the strength from somewhere to pop my lips and call me a blasphemer. But she would just scrunch her face up at me like I was buggin', purse her lips, roll her eyes, and look away. Other times I would share my deep reflections on a certain text in the Bible that I found problematic, and because my grandmother was mostly nonverbal due to her illness at this point, she would just quietly stare into my eyes and give a little brief nod as if to affirm that this was a valid question to be having as well.

It was nearly five years later before I came out as non-Christian to the rest of my family. The terror I had about not sharing the same truth system as they did kept me in the closet for years, beyond the time I had reconciled for myself that Jesus was a thing for me but Christianity was not. I use the language "came out" and "in the closet" because when I share this experience with my queer friends— the anxiety, the terror, the fear of rejection, and the loss of relationship that often happens when you "come out" as something other than what has been deemed socially acceptable for the community of folk who raised you—all of my beloved queer friends have said some version of, "Girl. That sounds like what it felt like to come out gay/lesbian/bisexual/queer/trans to my family." It was hard, and I'm still healing through some of the trauma of lost relationships as a result of my truth system.

Christianity is so important to so many Black people. It has been such a vital tool for liberation for Black folk, specifically Black American descendants of chattel slavery. I acknowledge the duplicity and complicated relationship Christianity and chattel slavery share because we largely became Christian due to the intentionality of slavers forcing conversion. Jesus became our everything because Jesus was offering freedom. Heaven became our everything because there was no way that we would be free in this body. However, the scripture that we had been hearing preached to us said that "to be absent from the body is to be present with the Lord." So Heaven was truly paradise—a literal place to be free—because there was no slavery in the Heaven being preached to the enslaved. We knew Jesus as the Savior of the world, and if you are a slave, of course, you need a savior.

Not identifying as a Christian, for many people who identify as Christian, automatically translates to, "You don't believe in Jesus," and not believing in Jesus means that you are going to hell. In the same way that many enslaved parents tried desperately to protect their families from the brutal violence of slavery, so do many Black Christian elders, parents, and "saved" folk resort to what some might perceive as extreme measures, desperate to protect their loved ones from going to hell. Being "saved," then, is protection from descending to hell, and this becomes a central tool by which Black people ensure freedom for themselves and their people.

Suppose you are a child of this indoctrination. In that case, there is an unspoken (often spoken) way that you must exist in this Christocentric society, particularly inside of a Black Christian experience that centers scripture, like, "Train up a child in the way he should go, and when he is old, he will not depart from it." The hope of this text is a desperate expectation that you can teach your children the way to stay alive by centering this religious truth system most specifically. That as long as they adhere to these Christian ideals and principles,

they will be safe, not just from the violence of the global white supremacist society we live in but also saved from hell. To tell my family,
particularly my parents, that I no longer identified as a Christian
translated for them as, "My child is going to hell," or "My child is not
safe from an eternal violence that is seeking to devour her daily—the
devil. In this metaphor, anti-Black, global white supremacy equals the
devil.

This chapter is not an attempt to downplay the transformative
power of Jesus Christ or the profound liberation, healing, and freedom
that can be found in a decolonized Christianity. Jesus is very important to me, and the confession of my faith is that Jesus was my way to
God. Additionally, Christianity does not belong to the slaver, especially since Christianity was on the continent of Africa before
European colonizers began using Christianity as a tool to harm and
force the ownership of an entire race of people. My theological shift,
in fact, is not a rejection of Jesus Christ, nor is it an assertion that
Black people are only Christian because of the gruesome violence of
slavery. However, my theological shift rejects the contemporary labeling of Christian because my truth system is rooted in the inherent
holiness of Blackness and the vital relationship with my ancestors and
their Black spiritual practices and technology—a spiritual technology
that predates any story of my people as not free. My theological truth
system, therefore, has space for both an African spiritual technology
and for the nappy-headed, brown-skinned, radical revolutionary
Christ called Jesus who was God-enfleshed and came to show the way
to Heaven/freedom.

My focus on ancestor veneration asserts that Jesus is, in fact, one of
my ancestors. I would never have the capacity to reject Jesus while
embracing ancestor reverence because Jesus is in that number, and I
call on him for wisdom and for help daily. Additionally, by reaching
for the spirituality of my ancestors, I also cannot throw Christianity

out with the bathwater because generations of my own blood relatives' spiritual practices include Christianity. I understand that this tradition has essential tools that also get me closer to freedom, which I understand as Heaven. There is no way for me to fully enflesh freedom, in this body, without both Jesus and the eternal spiritual wisdom of my elders, particularly the voice of my guiding ancestor, my grandmother, who was a Christian.

The Christian Demonic Filter insists that talking about any spiritual wisdom or technology outside of Jesus Christ is demonic, which makes it impossible for many Black people who identify as Christians to do ancestral healing work. "The Christian Demonic Filter" is a term I coined years before my theological shift. As a cultural anthropologist, I had questions about my observation of Black Christian people, raised with Southern Black Christian ethics, which are often very unique from other nonblack Christian people's expressions of their faith. For example, catching the holy ghost, running around the church, fainting, being slain in the spirit, and the way a certain chord played on the organ or the bass guitar at Sunday's service causes hysteria throughout the entire congregation are inherently Black behaviors but not specifically Christian. The Christian Demonic Filter is the internal spiritual judgment system that filters anything not expressly spelled out in the Bible as "demonic." Operating through the Western Christian lens, The Christian Demonic Filter categorizes Eastern religious and spiritual truth systems and Black deities as wicked or unholy. The Christian Demonic Filter, specifically, has a heavy filter on all things referring to anything culturally, traditionally, and historically Black as "demonic."

Somehow, The Christian Demonic Filter did not filter out the language of "old soul" or "that child been here before . . ." or "that baby born after Mama died is Mama," which, if contextualized in relation to spirituality, we might understand as "reincarnation." But that's not the point. The point is, The Christian Demonic Filter does not always have consistent doctrine across the board for Christians. The socialized nature of this filter frequently proves itself to be inherently anti-Black because there is either no scripture-based doctrine on which it can stand, or there is no historical contextualization of where the idea comes from in the first place.

Which brings us to ancestral reverence as a perfect example. Matthew started out the New Testament laying the groundwork to prove that Jesus is the Messiah to the Jewish people. He attempts this by detailing the lineage of Jesus Christ in Matthew 1:

> 1 The book of the generation of Jesus Christ, the son of David, the son of Abraham. 2 Abraham begat Isaac; and Isaac begat Jacob; and Jacob begat Judas and his brethren; 8 And Asa begat Josaphat; and Josaphat begat Joram; and Joram begat Ozias; 12 And after they were brought to Babylon, Jechonias begat Salathiel; and Salathiel begat Zorobabel; 16 And Jacob begat Joseph, the husband of Mary, of whom was born Jesus, who is called Christ. 17 So all the generations from Abraham to David are fourteen generations; and from David until the carrying away into Babylon are fourteen generations; and from the carrying away into Babylon unto Christ are fourteen generations.

Such and such begat so-and-so begat such and such begat Jesus. The bloodline of Jesus, as the Messiah, matters both spiritually and legally because in order to prove that the Messiah has come, there must be proof that the Lion of the Tribe of Judah has arrived, and that Lion must also be a descendant of David. The bloodline of Jesus matters because the bloodline has information about what is to come, and the bloodline of Jesus matters because the bloodline proves the legal right to inheritance.

Our ancestors matter because they have information about who we are and who we will be. They legally prove our inheritance. It's important not to reject the forever relationship between ourselves and our ancestors. They hold certain information that we will only have access to as a result of our relationship with them. Our ancestors ensure our legal access to what is rightfully ours—for example, reparations in the form of land, healthcare, education, and money.

My grandmother Emma Jane Baxley didn't have to pick cotton. In fact, she is the only one of her siblings that her sharecropper parents did not make pick cotton. Her mother said that she was "too smart," so my grandmother got to go to school. Because education became a powerful tool, it liberated my grandmother from levels of poverty that she might not have been able to escape if not for the opportunity given to her to learn. All of her children and grandchildren went to school. We benefited from the decision of my great-grandparents not to make my grandmother pick cotton and to allow her to go to school.

It feels very arrogant to assume that my great-grandmother Minnie Bell Lee never thought of me. Very presumptuous that she didn't ever look at her daughter Emma Jane and think about her daughter Carrie Kasandra, who begat me, EbonyJanice. And that feels so arrogant and presumptuous because I am always thinking about generations and generations and generations that have yet to form in my body. I think about them all the time. So why would my great-grandmother never have considered me?

My grandmother got to go to school.

So her daughter could go to school.

So her daughter (me) could build a school in Kenya.

The idea of never considering my ancestors would cut me off from everything that Minnie Bell Lee did when she seemingly arbitrarily said, "Emma is too smart. She cannot pick cotton. She will go to school." There is a moment in the bloodline of EbonyJanice Moore where someone looked into the future and saw me and said, "This is what we must do in order to ensure the inheritance of this family." The only way I get that information is through ancestral relationship and reverence.

Another reason why we must have an ongoing relationship with our ancestors is because, to heal forward, there is some backward generational healing that must happen. Think of the violence inside of our relationships being passed down from generation to generation with the excuse, "That's how my parents raised us."

I always use the example of the mother cutting the ends of the ham off before she puts it in the pan to cook in the oven.

"Why do you cut the ends of the ham off before you cook it?"

Mother says, "Because my mother used to cook her ham that way, and I learned to cook the ham from her."

"Grandmother, why did you cook the ham that way?"

Grandmother replies, "Because I didn't have a pan that was large enough for the ham."

For years, then, the mother was cooking her ham a particular way solely because her mother did it that way out of necessity. Having not contextualized that her mother did not have the same resources that she had, the mother added extra, unnecessary steps to her process that could have been avoided with more information from her mother.

The inability to contextualize both the information and resources available to your parents at that time and compare them to the information and resources available to you now is a trauma response. This trauma response leaves little room to say, "Just because my parents did this does not mean that I have to continue doing it. I am further in my familial freedom journey than my parents were at that time. I have more information and more access."

In order to heal our bloodline forward, we get to ask questions to our elders and our ancestors about the who, what, when, where, why, and how. But we know for many of us, we can only go so far back in our ancestry, especially if you happen to be adopted or orphaned. This means that you must be able to use the tool of spiritual imagination to have those essential conversations—and they are essential conversations. My womanist truth system will not allow me to believe that God has forgotten me just because I can only go so far back in my lineage, so there must be some mechanism through which I can access those records. As a descendant of enslaved people, my records either don't exist or only go back so far. But my spiritual tools can take me back as far as I need to go because I refuse to reject the eternal wisdom of the ancestors.

Additionally, our relationship with the ancestors has the potential to heal them. Years ago, after she started visiting me in dreams and visions seemingly out of nowhere, I started asking questions about my father's mother because while she was alive, in flesh, she didn't talk a lot. *Years of ancestral veneration later, I can't get her to stop being shady, talking from my altar now, but that's another book for another time.* But when she was in this flesh form, my grandmother Bernice Gully did not talk a lot. As I began to ask her children to tell me stories about her, what I found is that in less than three sentences, they would always start talking about their father and what their father did to their mother. Trauma. Without fail, I could ask an aunt something specific about her mother, and she would say two or three sentences about her mother, and before I knew it, we would be talking about something her father said or did. I would ask my father about his mother, and before I knew it, he would mention two or three sentences about his mother specifically, and then we would be back on the subject of his father.

One day, I was with my dad and his youngest brother in the same room, so to see if a group discussion about their mother would go the same way, I asked them about her at the same time. Two or three sentences combined, and their father immediately came up. I said, "Let me stop you right there. Do y'all realize that every time I ask y'all about your mother, you start talking about what your father did to her, and you never tell me the specific thing I'm asking about her?"

My uncle said, "You know what? I never realized that. But it makes sense that we do that because there is so much trauma. It's hard to talk about that time without thinking about the trauma."

That is when I realized that, both in my grandmother's life and in her passing, she was known for her trauma. What my grandmother needed from me was for somebody, anybody, to say her name without mentioning her trauma. It makes sense that she would come to me in dreams and visions because I am probably one of the few people in our family willing to have a conversation on behalf of an ancestor. So that's what I did. I took the one story my aunt could share with me about the time she saw a photo of my grandmother as a teenager in New Orleans at a bar with her cousin. She said that my grandmother looked so young, fresh, and content in the picture. My aunt begged her cousin to let her have a copy of the photo, but it ended up being destroyed in Hurricane Katrina. So, even though I would never be able to see the photo myself, I took that tiny bit of story and used my spiritual imagination to fill in the blanks or holes in my grandmother's story. My spiritual imagination allowed me to tell the whole story of my grandmother as a teenager at a bar with her cousin. In the spirit realm, using my spiritual imagination, I am able to heal my grandmother of some of her trauma. In this story that I wrote in my journal, my grandmother was still shy but giggled her way through the night as young men approached her and her cousin to ask them to dance or try to get them to run off with them. I described my grandmother as a "fine, young tenderoni," and at the end of the story, she is "grinning herself silly" for the rest of the night.

A few days later, my oldest sister came into the room where my altar was and saw the photo of my grandmother there and said, "You know, I've never looked at that photo before and thought she looked happy, but since you put that photo of her on your altar, she looks like she is grinning." I got goose bumps on my arms when she said the word "grinning" because it felt like an affirmation from my grandmother that just by saying her name and telling a story about her that had something to do with her as a woman worthy of grinning and giggling, I had healed something in my bloodline. This healing wasn't just a backward healing, though, because not only do I refuse to let people talk about my grandmother as solely her trauma any longer but my generation, forward, also now has language for "Do not talk about me as if I am only my trauma." We cannot afford to forsake the relationship with our ancestors because healing them also heals us.

Dr. Brittney Cooper gives us language for this kind of Black feminist/womanist evolving where our spirituality is concerned. In her book *Eloquent Rage*, she calls this "Grown Woman Theology." Grown Woman Theology is the personal theology we develop for ourselves once we have intentionally and consciously interrogated the religious beliefs and theories of our youth that often held us in bondage or did not see us as whole. Grown Woman Theology gives us the chance to ask, "Is that my voice?" "Is that my belief?" "Is that really true for me?" It also holds space to reflect on the difference between the preachment of our youth and the actual lived theology of our elders. Dr. Cooper gives the example of being in her early twenties when her grandmother took her to the side to tell her it was time for her to have some good sex, even though she wasn't married. This conversation was a gateway for her own realization that she had deeply internalized certain ideas that weren't true for her or many of the free women around her. Grown Woman Theology is important because it gives you language to contribute to the community of faith amongst whom you are growing, and it is vital because it affirms you as a whole person and a worthy contributor to your own, individual definition of your faith and freedom. (Committed to the survival and wholeness of entire people . . . Not a separatist, except periodically, for health.)

Ancestral reverence is a major liberation tool that Black people, specifically Black women and girls in the context of this book, are returning to because we understand that healing our ancestors is one of the ways we heal ourselves. We used language like "breaking generational curses." I love the way that Zakiyyah Abdul-Mateen offers that "breaking generational curses is too hard," and we deserve to not have to always be doing hard work. She counters that a "forever ancestral healing" journey is more gentle language for our nervous systems, and committing to the forever journey of healing is how we reach for the tools our ancestors were always showing us. Ancestral healing reveals and helps mend generational trauma. The simple act of acknowledging our ancestors may help heal grief and give us language for our own Grown Woman Theology.

Pursuing our ancestors is a radical and revolutionary tool because our ancestors affirm our right to softness, loudness, madness, and wellness. They honor us with wisdom through our dreams and want, desperately, for us to own our names and our bodies so that we might be able to live in the unashamedness that many of them did not have a right to pursue. Simply, pursuing my ancestors is my activism because it makes me more me, and that makes me freer.

IN PURSUIT OF
AUTHORITY

"I'm not a biter, I'm a writer for myself and others.
I say a B.I.G. verse, I'm only biggin' up my brother."

—JAY-Z

Once upon a time, in a land steeped in white supremacy, a white Quaker female minister published a book. The title was stolen from a Black femme named Sesali Bowen. The theory is literally my hip-hop womanist theory, which happens to be public scholarship that I've been building and contributing to for the last seven years. It is important to note that, yes, she absolutely did follow me on social media. So, yes, she absolutely knew of my work, and no, you not finna convince me that this was a coincidence. Also, in this land far, far away from reality, she did not cite me or Sesali Bowen, the Black femme from whom she stole her title. Nor did she cite any of the other brilliant Black femmes who have been asking the questions she claimed to be asking in her li'l pamphlet. Additionally, she received a whole grant from thee Yale University to "write" this book, and a cute li'l book deal from Wipf and Stock Publishers. Nobody in either of those institutions ever thought it was a good idea to say, "This is a bad idea."

You've heard this story before. It is a tale as old as time. It's called, "colonization." Something already exists, but a white person pulls up on the territory and puts a flag down in the middle of someone's front yard and says, "Behold, I have discovered this person, place, thing, or idea!" This particular colonizer claimed to be "building" an ethic that I and other Black feminist and womanist scholars centering hip-hop in our contribution to canon-building already built, and most impressively, even with the blueprint sitting right there in her face, she still did it awfully. You know why? Because colonizers don't have to do the thing that already exists better in order to take ownership of it; the mere nature of their claim and their whiteness offers them a power and authority where they are not credible at all.

Authority: "the power or right to give orders, to make decisions, to enforce obedience. A person, organization, or institution that has political or administrative power or control."

The day after Beyoncé was snubbed for Album of the Year for her sixth studio album, *Lemonade*, her sister Solange Knowles tweeted a series of now-deleted tweets that ended with the words, "Be the gold you want to hold, my G." At that time in my life, I was about to apply for a TED fellowship, and I saw that tweet. It made me think of how few Black women I had seen on the main TED stage at that point. The TED organization brings lecturers, thought leaders, teachers, educators, and creatives to the table and gives them a platform, essentially acknowledging them as an authority on their subject matter. This platform has opened many doors and propelled many TED participants into other spaces where that speaker can be considered the authority on their subject matter. When I thought about "Be the gold you want to hold, my G," I thought to myself, *Who authorized TED 'nem? Who said that TED 'nem were in charge and that they should be the authorizing agency or body through which we deem whoever's on that stage more credible or more worthy to speak on that topic?* Historically, TED hasn't had an equitable number of Black women on their main stage. Yes, I know hella Black women who have done city-organized TEDx talks, but TEDx is not TED. And that matters.

A question that kept coming up for me was, "What would it look like if we divested from the self-appointed authorizing agency?" This is where I got the language of "decolonizing authority" to withdraw from the governing authority with the goal of self-determination and sovereignty. Decolonizing authority is a conversation about power dynamics and is important to revolution, resistance, movement, and our activism because one would have to heal themselves from the idea of being subordinate in order to truly inherit their divine right to be seen as credible and free.

This is why I founded "Black Girl Mixtape," originally a multi-platform lecture series created to center the intellectual authority of Black women. Too many conversations were happening where Black women were excluded from the panel, the discussion, the anthology, or the board. Often, even conversations on the topic of Black woman-hood happen without Black women at the table (e.g., the colonizer who wrote the book claiming to "build towards" an ethic on the topic of Black womanhood that Black women had already built). Another example that felt very personal to me was how often hip-hop conversations were happening, and somehow, there were no Black women at a table we helped build.

Our absence in so many spaces made me think a lot about authority and credibility.

Question number one: Who authorized these folk?

Question number two: Without Black women's contributions, are they really credible?

Black Girl Mixtape started as a lecture series simply creating space for Black women and femmes to speak from a place of authority on the work of their soul. Other Black women, then, became the mirror for these lecturers to see themselves lifted and centered as credible and worthy. Eventually, Black Girl Mixtape evolved into a "multi-platform safe think space centering the creative and intellectual authority of Black women." We are a collaborative of writers, thinkers, healers, scholars, and creatives focused on all issues pertaining to Black womanhood. We are doing the deep work of diasporic healing by affirming and centering ourselves in discussions that require Black women's contribution in order to be whole, holy, and full.

I built Black Girl Mixtape by focusing on three major tenets that both authorize and make me credible to be doing the work I do in the world. My education, my lived experience, and my ancestors qualify me, authorize me, and amplify me. These three tenets are called "The Range." Anytime a Black woman questions her credibility in any space she is in, I ask the question, "Do you have The Range?" And this isn't just for some corporate, professional, or academic space. This question, "Do you have The Range," is for whoever you are and wherever you are in your work, sis. We are leaders and revolutionary when it comes to framework and praxis because we have always walked it like we talk it. Meaning, that degree you got from the School of Hard Knocks is your authorization. The combination of education, lived experience, and our ancestors' blessing is what makes us top-tier authority on us, our history, our legacy, and beyond. Even before we had the language of theory, praxis, or ethic, we had theory, praxis, and ethic.

I had been doing cultural anthropological research and deep spiritual archaeological digs long before I got a degree in cultural anthropology, took any archaeology classes, or even considered seminary. When I was ten years old, I studied the lyrics in Bone Thugs-N-Harmony's "1st of tha Month" line by line and precept by precept. I wanted to memorize and ask questions about the lyrics to satisfy my curiosity about this experience I knew very little about. That was a form of music ethnography. When I was sneaking into my grandmother's front room to pull out each piece of jewelry, putting on the rings, the clip-on earrings, and the long beaded necklaces and closing my eyes to imagine the story behind each of those items, that is what Dr. Clarissa Pinkola Estés calls "psychic archaeological digs." And when I was sitting with my elders, one-on-one, to ask them questions about their stories, old wives' tales, folk sayings, plant medicines, and denominational variations of their religious practices, documenting these stories in my journals and incorporating that language into my own lived experiences that is both ethnography and participant-observation research, did I have the language for that then? Of course not. Does that make my fieldwork or my findings any less credible? Absolutely not.

Colonized authority is white male hierarchical. Essentially, there were some old white men, years ago, who said, "This is the superior process, theory, and methodology that is credible. These are the standards by which one is able to enter into this space and be deemed credible. This is the authorizing body through which one will have to enter in order to be deemed credible." Here we are, years later, still sitting around here in agreement. That is silly at best, violent at worst. It's easy to see why that's problematic. First of all, do we really trust what some old, dead white man said about authority? This is what we're doing? Secondly, we live in the land of patriarchal white supremacist delusion. It's easy to understand why even gaining access to the so-called authorizing body is nearly impossible for marginalized folk, especially based on the various intersectional identities of those bodies. Also, the standard itself is steeped in misogyny and racism. To still be reaching for that as the credible practice of authorization in this the year of our Lord Fantasia Barrino is a crime. Another vital question is, "Who authorized the authority?" Decolonizing authority can be as simple as asking that question, and it could be as revolutionary as saying, "I reject that."

The framework that I call "The Range" gives us a decolonized idea of how we look to authority and credibility in a nonwhite, male-centered hierarchical way. While formal education may be central to a colonized authorizing agency, a decolonized authority centers education as one of its tenets by asking, "What kind of education?" because there are various ways to receive an education. Yes, I have all these little degrees, but also, I've been the secretary of the Sunday school at New Jerusalem Missionary Baptist Church since I was eight years old. I have been preaching from the pulpit since I was eight years old. I have studied and apprenticed under brilliant thinkers, theologians, and Bible scholars from birth. I have been teaching Sunday school since I was six years old. I literally learned how to make my first lesson plan at the feet of my grandmother Emma Jane Baxley, to be the student teacher of the baby class at age six. I have been trained in public speaking since I was old enough to speak and memorize the words, "Jesus rose. Happy Easter."

To suggest that my education begins at which point I enroll in some institution, in a formal capacity, is to assert that all of this training prior to this moment of so-called credible and formal education is not valid or essential to what I will contribute in the "formal" setting.

The educational tenet wants to discredit our personal time and lived experience, even though it contributes to your social, political, and professional capacity. What is the "informal" training that you didn't deem worthy of adding to your CV, your cover letter, or your resume? Meanwhile, you have been learning at the feet of your Big Mama for thirty-plus years, and when a colonized authorizing agency suggests that you need X number of years of experience to have access to that space, it never crosses your mind that your time with Big Mama could be phrased in such a way that it reveals your years of knowledge and experience on that subject matter.

You also have devalued your so-called informal education and experience to make you feel like an imposter. This is important to note because when I say my education is one of the tenets of my authority and a decolonized conversation around authority, I do not want to suggest that this is just because I went from Hancock Elementary to Mills Middle School to Jackson Junior High School to all these little colleges I attended, and that education is what makes me credible. No. I have always been learning in and out of various forms of both traditional and nontraditional spaces, and all of that learning contributes to my education and my credibility.

Womanism also gives us a knowing of this reality because womanists believe that we co-create knowledge in community. That means that sometimes when my girlfriends and I are just talking about life and being random and frivolous, something profound happens, and knowledge is co-created. Our combined knowing created some new information, and there is no so-called *formal institution* that values the brilliance of our co-creation. Even without language for it, we have historically, in a communal way, appreciated deep, decolonized educational realities (think of book-smart versus street-smart conversations).

LIVED EXPERIENCE

My lived experience qualifies me, authorizes me, and deems me credible because I did it already, so my life is the proof of my capacity and my credibility. From a churchy perspective, we might call this our testimony, and our testimony is the proof of what happened and what we were capable of. This church perspective also decolonizes a white male–centered authority because it would consider God the authorizing agency that proved the capacity and credibility. From a hip-hop perspective, Jay-Z would say, "Nobody in [rap] did it quite like I did it. If you did it, I done it before, you get it, I had it. Got mad at it and don't want it no more . . . Get it right, did different, did it better, did it nice. Did the impossible, then did it twice." Hip-hop is consistently citing the lived experience as the proof and bragging that, "I showed you how to do this, son" (Jay-Z).

In a traditional academic setting, this lived experience piece would be deemed credible if it was filtered through a social scientist, ethnography, participant observation, or any other cultural anthropological methodology. This usually means it will require someone who is not a part of the culture being studied to observe and detail the different portions of the culture, customs, and behaviors in order for that culture and those customs to be deemed credible markers for understanding the people, the place, or the thing. That is a colonized way of understanding "lived experience" as a credible tool for legitimizing information. To decolonize that practice is to say, "I am both participating and observing, and I am credible with or without a degree."

Hip-hop historian Dr. Kashema Hutchinson gives us language for this when she compares Meek Mill as a critical race theorist with the bunch of white social theorists who have been affirmed as credible scholars in this field. She does this by creating infographics that lay out Meek Mill lyrics next to the theories of those old, dead, white male scholars. Then she asks the question, "If Meek Mill is saying this in his lyrics while just detailing his lived experience, why would we say that this old white man is more credible to detail this theory than the one living it?" It's profound to see her break down these lyrics and consider the ethical issue of considering one more credible than the other. That is the work that I have been doing for years—comparing hip-hop lyrics with sacred text and asking why one is more credible than the other. Dr. Hutchinson proves, with these infographics, that these artists have a profound understanding of the so-called intellectual framework laid out by these old white men. Even if they've never studied or call it what these old white men called it, their life in relation to these ideas makes them credible.

Ancestors are a very essential tenet in this framework that I call "The Range." This is a major part of the reason why ancestral healing and veneration is essential to this revolutionary living and existing of Black girlhood, because without the consideration of who I am and what I know solely because of the ancestors, I'm missing out on a piece of the puzzle that affirms me as worthy, whole, and credible. I always say that I have friends who know things that they cannot know. My friend Bettyna Turner says, "How did you think that with your brain?" because that's how profound the thought process can be. How did you even get your brain to arrive at that profound thought? What I know for sure is *that* is spirit. That is generational knowledge passed down either through story or through blood.

My grandmother's mother, Minnie Bell Lee, also known as Madea, transitioned to the eternal when my mother was a child, which means I never met her. But I have told stories to my grandmother and my mother about their mother that had them sitting looking at me like, "Girl. How do you know this? It is impossible for you to know this." But I know it.

Thea Monyeé wrote a book called *Blood & Bajareque* about ancestors that she has never met and the family very rarely discusses. She wrote about elders from different continents that she had never met and customs in the bloodline that no one ever discussed because those traditions were deemed taboo. When her parents read her book, their minds were blown because there was no way for her to know those things. Additionally, when I read the book for the first time, even though she was speaking about her own ancestral knowing, so much of what she wrote mirrored ideas and realities that I had not yet found the language to explain of my own ancestral knowing. There is no formal educational institution that can teach you that, so to solely be reliant on an external authorizing agency to deem you worthy and credible as an authority on a thing that you can only know because the ancestors revealed it, whispered it, passed it down through their bloodline, showed up in a dream, a vision, or a knowing is to invalidate the brilliant thing that you know for a fact that you know.

Often, because that casually brilliant ancestral knowing does not have some external validation or explanation, this contributes to the imposter syndrome that you experience on an ongoing basis as a Black woman and girl doing casually brilliant work in the world. You struggle with insecurity and imposter syndrome because those so-called authorized institutions make everything harder than it has to be in order to erase and gate-keep the spaces. So you have gone a lifetime asking yourself, "Is this good enough because it seems to come too easy for me? Everybody else is hustling and bustling and struggling. Maybe I should be putting more effort into this." Sister, why would you have to put more effort into the thing that is just in your bones? Why should you have to put more effort into the thing that is just growing out of your head? How could you ever put more effort into the things that are crisscrossed in the lines of your fingerprints? No. Your ancestors make you credible, authorize you, affirm you, and secure you.

THE SPARK DESERVES CITATION

When legal scholar Richard Delgado coined the term "Politics of Citation" and said that "citation is political," he was pointing to the exclusion of minority scholars of civil rights by white scholars who co-opted the field for themselves (because colonizers been colonizing from age to age and generation to generation). As we continue to be in relationship with the language of "the politics of citation," we realize that we have political power with our intentionality around citation. This looks like building classes with solely Black women and femme authors as a way to subvert the standardized white-centered curriculum full of articles, books, and research of the white scholars deemed credible by the white-centered authorizing agency.

Citation is political and also looks like building a deep ethic of citation, at all times, in all spaces, because we understand that when knowledge is being shared, it is easy to erase Black women and femmes from the discussion, even when we were the ones who introduced the language. If I had a dollar for every time I was personally quoted without being cited, I would have a whole lot of dollars. So the ethic of citation is political because when we include the source of our knowledge in our discussions, we ensure that person is not erased, and we also make ourselves more credible by acknowledging our intellectual lineage.

Years ago, Muslim poet, rapper, and activist Mona Haydar told me that for Muslims it's basically a sin not to cite your sources. If someone were speaking about Allah, Muslims would ask questions like, "What is your spiritual (or intellectual) lineage?" "What prophet said that?" "What teacher taught you that?" "Where did you get that information from?" She and I were having this conversation because I was telling her that I believe that if I am having a conversation with someone and they say something that leads my train of thought to a different subject, that person deserves citation because whatever they said was the spark to my thought, and therefore, they are a part of my "intellectual lineage." Hence my idea that "the spark deserves citation."

The spark is a part of my intellectual lineage. The spark makes me more credible. Citing the spark makes intellect communal, which is womanist, which is right! APA, MLA, Chicago 'n' nem may not have a format for citing the spark, but womanism does. "When I was talking to (insert person's name), they said ABC, and that made me think about XYZ (and then I continue on with my explanation of XYZ)." I do not leave a conversation where a spark for another thought arrives without tracing the breath of the thought. And then, I do that every single time I speak. This ensures people don't walk away from a conversation where I'm quoting Maya Angelou thinking that EbonyJanice is the one who said the caged birds be singing.

I also do this every single time I speak because citation is political in that it ensures there aren't a bunch of people in the world talking about Black girl ish, and none of the Black girls are getting any of the credit or reaping any of the benefits. Think about the ways social media makes it so possible to steal the intellectual and creative contributions of others daily. All you have to do is repost the quote with the author's name and social media handle, as it was. Instead, people re-create the thing that already exists and try to pass it off as their own. A perfect example of this happened in 2020 when the choreography for a TikTok dance called "Renegade" went viral, and several white girls reposted themselves doing the choreography, got major brand deals, were invited to late-night shows to do the dance on television, and one of these white girls ended up in a Super Bowl commercial. Black social media had to threaten a civil war to get the originator of that dance, Jalaiah Harmon, any credit for the thing that she created that was the springboard for other people's rise to celebrity and success and not her own. While Jalaiah's name has been lifted, and she is now noted as the creator of this dance craze, she still never received the level of recognition that the young white girls who re-created her creation, poorly, without simply "citing their source," received. Is there anything wrong with a repost? Absolutely not. But to erase the source is to suggest that you created, founded, invented, and ideated a thing that you had no capacity to do without the contribution of your intellectual or creative lineage. Just like I want Jalaiah to get her flowers, I want all the Black girls to get the flowers they deserve. Every. Single. Time.

Here's the reality of decolonizing authority by being intentional with your citation. You assert and affirm that you have a deep well of wisdom from which you source everything you are claiming. I did not think of this book by myself. When you hear from me, you're hearing from my guiding ancestors who were also healers and scholars: Zora Neale Hurston, Toni Morrison, Maya Angelou, Veronika Seaborn, Aduni Idowu, Emma Jane Baxley, and Bernice Gully. When you hear from me, you are hearing from everything I know because of Kasandra Moore, Jessica Nycole Ralph, Nikki Blak, Sonya Renee Taylor, Mahogany L. Browne, Zakiyyah Abdul-Mateen, Chiara Richardson, Imara Jones, Belinda Joyce Styles, Emmico McCarty, Tara Mixon, Alesha Baxley, Baryl Miller, Cortney Bohannon, Khadijah Abdul-Mateen, Candace Simpson, Lynette Baxley, Jade T. Perry, Phyllis Brantley, Shawntelle Willis, Viola McKinney, Raquel Willis, Pat Matthews, Sherma Shoemo, Denise Warren, Jaha Zainabu, Joyce Lee, Bettyna Turner, Tamela Julia Gordon, Toni-Michelle Williams, Jacqueline Banks, Roya Marsh, Vernitha Fearon, Alysa Hutchinson, Trina Cooper, Alystia Nicole Moore, Nirel Jones Mitchell, Tameeka Galloway, D'dra White, Jamie Matthews, Oprah Winfrey, Katrice Mines, Dawn Willis, Danee Black, Aria Sa'id, Queen Latifah, and of course, Beyoncé Giselle Knowles-Carter.

The idea that we will undervalue our profound contribution to the world, while the world undervalues our contribution to the world, and we sit over here feeling like imposters in the meantime is a strong "No" for me. In the words of our auntie Iyanla Vanzant, *slams hand on table*, "Not on my watch!"

ACKNOWLEDGMENTS

The first book I ever self-published was a book of poems called *Young Black Girl* (see the consistency with the Black-girl theme). I was nineteen/twenty years old, and I knew nothing about publishing, so I did everything myself. And then my parents bought me a laser printer. This may sound very basic, but this was back when printers cost a house note and paper cost a light bill. I printed the pages, bound the book with staples and a glue gun, and proudly sold that book on MySpace for ten dollars under my own imprint called Belle Noire Publishing. I want to thank my parents, Jacob and Kasandra Moore, for the spaciousness that your participation in my forever folly has always created for me to dream. I do not make sense to you most of the time, but you still hold out your arms with grace and love until the vision comes alive. Thank you!

To my aunt Viola McKinney and my aunt Phyllis Brantley, thank you for the audacity you demonstrate by believing I can do anything. It's hilarious to watch the two of you claim me as your own and try to out-cheer the world for me! A book about womanism doesn't exist without mentioning the way you love and celebrate me.

To my sister Alesha Baxley, asking me what this book is about every time we speak has made my thirty-second book pitch supreme. Thank you for that, girl! Nobody loves me like you!

To my oldest sister, Lynette Baxley, your support for me is unmatched. I'm funnier because of you. I'm bolder because of you. I'm more confident because of you. And I make braver moves because you see me so possible. Thank you and I love you too much, Plynne!

There are so many people to acknowledge for how a book like *All the Black Girls Are Activists* comes to exist. I will not list my friends because that's a missed name waiting to happen, and I bet y'all not finna be mad with me. So, to ALL of you, thank you. I love you. I mean it. You know it. There is no confusion on this fact.

I must acknowledge my publisher, Rebekah Borucki, for how a DM conversation on IG turned into a partnership and a book deal ten days later. You are the proof of decolonized publishing. I am in awe of the way you dream us all more possible, and I will never have all the words to express my gratitude for your grace throughout this process. This would be a completely different book anywhere else. Thank you!

Tamela Julia Gordon, my editor and sister-friend. What was this book before you? You asked me questions, graciously and shadily, that challenged everything I imagined this work could be. Me and you are Nettie and Celie. Ain't no ocean, ain't no sea that could keep me from, at least, asking you with roses, champagne, a slow R&B begging playlist, and some confetti to do this book thing with me again and again! I could not have thought this book without you. Thank you!

Danielle Gant, you are the MVP with the way you turned around the final proofreading notes for this book in such a short amount of time. Thank you for every comma, deleted space, and suggestion to rethink a sentence. Who knew sharing a library card with you for the last ten years would make this moment possible? God did!

To Bettyna Turner for helping me think with my brain on the days when I would have just lain in the bed and read a romance novel, come marvel with me forever at what joy we create as smart Black girls for life! Thank you a million trillion times.

ACKNOWLEDGMENTS

To my nieces, Aniya, Shanasia, Sakari, Trinity, Unique, and Oliviayona, I'm always thinking of you when I think of a safe world for the free Black girl to thrive. Each of you is my muse. I love you too much!

To my favorite person in the multiverse, thinking of the way you have rearranged me, genuinely and sincerely, makes me think of liberation every single day. I want to know the most free version of myself so I can focus all my light on love and only love. Everything else is a distraction. This is my favorite form of activism: tryna figure out how to be a bird, the wind, and a tree. Thank you for the revolution of your knowing.

To every Black girl on the planet, I wrote this in English as a Black American woman, but this book is because of and for all of you. Nuance and contextualize yourself throughout these pages and dream yourself free. Thank you for how you inspire me. (#Bars)

When I say I am a womanist, I mean that from my soul. I love us, for real.

WORKS CITED

Adams, Carol J., ed. *Ecofeminism and the Sacred.* Continuum, 1993.

Bailey, Moya. *Misogynoir Transformed: Black Women's Digital Resistance.* New York University Press, 2021.

Brown, Adrienne Maree. "Vegas and Everything Else." *Adrienne Maree Brown* (blog), October 2, 2017, https://adriennemareebrown.net/2017/10/02/vegas-and-everything-else/.

Coleman, Monica A. *Ain't I a Womanist, Too?: Third-Wave Womanist Religious Thought.* Fortress Press, 2013.

Cooper, Brittney C. *Eloquent Rage: A Black Feminist Discovers Her Superpower.* Picador, 2018.

Davis, Angela. "Reflections on the Black Woman's Role in the Community of Slaves." *Journal of Black Studies and Research* (1971): 3–15.

Estés, Clarissa Pinkola. *Women Who Run with the Wolves: Myths and Stories of the Wild Woman Archetype.* Ballantine Books, 1989.

Fleming, Olivia. "Rachel Cargle Insists Rest Is the Real Revolution for Black Women," *Harper's BAZAAR*, November 6, 2019, https://www.harpersbazaar.com/culture/politics/a29564338/rachel-cargle-women-who-dare/.

Gates Jr., Henry Louis. "The Black Church." Public Broadcasting Service, 2021, https://www.pbs.org/show/black-church/.

The Greenville News. "Negro Women To Be Put To Work," October 2, 1918.

Gyasi, Yaa. *Homegoing.* Vintage Books, 2017.

Higginbotham, Evelyn Brooks. *Righteous Discontent: The Women's Movement in the Black Baptist Church.* Harvard University Press, 1993.

Hurston, Zora Neale. *Their Eyes Were Watching God.* Virago Press, 2018.

Kelley, Robin D.G. *Freedom Dreams: The Black Radical Imagination.* Beacon Press, 2022.

Khan-Cullors, Patrisse, and Asha Bandele. *When They Call You a Terrorist: A Black Lives Matter Memoir.* St. Martin's Press, 2018.

King, Jamilah. "Uzo Aduba Never Thought about Changing Her Nigerian Name," *Colorlines*, June 25, 2014, https://colorlines.com/article/uzo-aduba-never-thought-about-changing-her-nigerian-name/.

Morgan, Joan. *When Chickenheads Come Home to Roost: A Hip-Hop Feminist Breaks It Down*. Simon & Schuster, 2017.

Morrison, Toni. "Toni Morrison: The Site of Memory." *Morrison_memory*, 1995, https://public.wsu.edu/~hughesc/morrison_memory.htm.

Phillips, Rasheedah. *Black Quantum Futurism. Theory and Practice*. Afrofuturist Affair/House of Future Sciences Books, 2021.

Townes, Emilie Maureen. *Womanist Ethics and the Cultural Production of Evil*. Palgrave Macmillan, 2006.

Walker-Barnes, Chanequa. *Too Heavy a Yoke: Black Women and the Burden of Strength*. Cascade Books, 2014.

Walker, Alice. *Anything We Love Can Be Saved: A Writer's Activism*. Phoenix, 2005.

Walker, Alice. *In Search of Our Mother's Gardens*. Harcourt Brace Jovanovich, 1983.

INDEX

ABOUT THE AUTHOR

EBONYJANICE is a dynamic lecturer, transformational speaker, passionate multifaith preacher, and creative focused on Decolonizing Authority, Hip-Hop Scholarship, Womanism as a Political and Spiritual/Religious tool for Liberation, Blackness as Religion, Dialogue as central to professional development and personal growth, and Women and Gender Studies focused on Black girlhood. She is also the founder of Black Girl Mixtape, a multiplatform, safe think-space centering the intellectual and creative authority of Black women, and Dream Yourself Free, a Spiritual Mentoring project focused on Black women's healing, dreaming, ease, play, and wholeness as their activism and resistance work.